ISLAND
OF
RIVERS

ISLAND
OF
RIVERS

AN ANTHOLOGY CELEBRATING
50 YEARS OF
OLYMPIC NATIONAL PARK

*Edited by Nancy Beres,
Mitzi Chandler & Russell Dalton*

Published by
Pacific Northwest National Parks & Forests Association
83 S. King Street, Suite 212, Seattle, WA 98104

Printed in the United States of America

92 91 90 89 88   5 4 3 2 1

ISBN 0-914019-18-X

Cover photograph: "Olympic National Park:
View from Blue Mountain" by Pat O'Hara

Table of contents

Explorations

Controversy

Pioneers

Wilderness

Memoirs

Acknowledgements

For permission to reprint all works in this volume by the following contributors, grateful acknowledgment is made to the holders of copyright, publishers or representatives named below and on the following pages.

"The Pulse of the Seasons," "The Early Exploration of the Olympic Peninsula," by Robert Wood. From *Trail Country*. Copyright 1968 by The Mountaineers, Seattle, WA. Reprinted by permission of The Mountaineers.

"Anniversary," by Frances Fagerlund. From *Tidepools* and *Sometimes the Words Cross Over*. Copyright 1986 Frances Fagerlund. Reprinted by permission of Frances Fagerlund.

"For the Boy Who Was Dodger Point Lookout Fifteen Years Ago," by Gary Snyder. From *The Backcountry*. Copyright 1968 by Gary Snyder. Reprinted by permission of New Directions Publishing Corp.

"Pole of Remoteness," by Harvey Manning. From *Washington Wilderness: The Unfinished Work*. Copyright 1984 by The Mountaineers, Seattle, WA. Reprinted by permission of The Mountaineers.

"Origin of Lake Crescent," "Thunderbird and Whale", "How Kwatee Made the Rivers and Rocks." From *Indian Legends of the Pacific Northwest*, by Ella E. Clark. Copyright 1953 by The Regents of the University of California. Copyright renewed 1981 by Ella Clark. Reprinted by permission of the University of California Press.

"Tale of Two Seas," by Tim McNulty. From *Olympic National Park, Where the Mountain Meets the Sea*. Copyright 1984 by Woodlands Press, San Rafael, CA. Reprinted by permission of Tim McNulty.

"Place Names of the Olympic National Park," by Smitty Parratt. From *Gods and Goblins*. Copyright 1984 by Smitty Parratt. Reprinted by permission of Smitty Parratt.

"Breaking New Ground," by Gifford Pinchot. From *Breaking New Ground*. Copyright 1945 by Harcourt Brace Jovanovich, Inc. Reprinted by permission of Gifford B. Pinchot, M.D.

"Pioneers of the Olympics," by Lois Crisler. From *The Pacific Coast Ranges*. Vanguard Press, NY, edited by Robert Peattie. Copyright 1946 by Robert Peattie. Reprinted by permission of Vanguard Press, Inc.

"Trees of Timberline," "The Alpine Flower Gardens," by E. B. Webster. From The Friendly Mountain. Copyright 1921 by E. B. Webster. Reprinted by permission of the *Peninsula Daily News.*

"The Olympic Backcountry Is Sleeping Safe in Snow," by Phyllis Miletich. From the *Port Angeles Daily News.* Reprinted by permission of Phyllis Miletich.

"Meditation above Ozette," by Tim McNulty. From *Pawtracks.* Copyright 1978 by Tim McNulty. Reprinted by permission of Tim McNulty.

"Pack Train Grandma," by Marian Taylor. Published in *Dalmo'ma,* under the title, "Pack Train Grandmother." Copyright 1984 by Marian Taylor. Reprinted by permission of Empty Bowl.

"Three Prune Creek," by Rudo Fromme. From *Memoirs of Rudo Fromme.* Copyright by Eleanor Fromme. Reprinted by permission of Eleanor Fromme.

"Near Kalaloch," by Richard Hugo. From *Making Certain It Goes On, Collected Poems.* Copyright 1984 by W. W. Norton & Co. Reprinted by permission of W. W. Norton & Co.

"Last Day of Summer on Hurricane Ridge," by Frances Fagerlund. From *Sometimes the Words Cross Over.* Copyright 1986 by Frances Fagerlund. Reprinted by permission of Frances Fagerlund.

We wish to express appreciation and gratitude to the following:
Jack Estes, Jerry Gorsline, Serena Lesley, Tim McNulty and Edward Tisch for the time and talents they brought to the Olympic National Park Anthology Committee; to Alice Hammer for the hours spent at the keyboard and for her invaluable creative input; to Richard Hammer for help with computer work; to the Webster Foundation; to Mary Ellen Rutter and the Pacific Northwest National Parks & Forests Association who provided the funding for this anthology; to Pat O'Hara for the cover photograph; to Olympic National Park for use of their copy machine and to Fran Andrews and Charlotte Arrodondo for the time spent copying anthology material; to John Teichert for the map of the Olympic National Park; to Randy Jones and Don Jackson for editorial input; to Robert Chandler for acting as liaison between the editorial committee and the PNNPFA; to Senator Dan Evans for his constant and continuous support of Olympic National Park; to the park visitor—past, present and future— whose spirit is rekindled in the solitude of Olympic's mountains, rain forests and ocean beaches.

You, as readers, may notice several pieces in this anthology that do not conform to current standards of grammar, spelling and punctuation. We, as editors, out of respect due these as valuable historical works, decided to let them stand as they did in their own time and would wish them appreciated in that context.

Nancy Beres
Mitzi Chandler
Russell Dalton

Foreword

In 1988, we celebrate the golden anniversary of Olympic National Park, established in 1938. As we honor this richly diverse park, we should reflect also on the history of the Olympic Peninsula and recall those intrepid explorers who first ventured into the vast wilderness of what is now the park nearly a century ago.

Early seafarers first viewed these glorious mountains from afar as they approached Washington's Pacific Coast. Later, explorers would investigate the majesty of the Olympics.

Lieutenant Joseph O'Neil and his young comrades sought to answer many intriguing questions and to resolve the mysteries of the Olympics. They struggled through massive virgin forests, clambered over rocky cliffs enraptured by the new vistas they saw from each mountain pass. The myths and speculation about these mountains evaporated before a reality more exalted than any dream. An ocean of uncut timber spilled over the river valleys that zigzagged in every direction. Rugged mountain peaks stood together like sentinels, their shoulders covered with glaciers that flowed closer to the sea than anywhere in the continental United States.

Even then the perceptive O'Neil recognized the value of the peninsula for a national park. In December of 1890, he gave an illustrated presentation in Portland, Oregon, of his exploration of the Olympics. He ended his narration with these words: "It has no geysers but every other requisite for a national park, as many wonders and natural beauties can be found in any localities, and it is today the last home of the noble elk, where he is to be found untamed and fearless of man. In a few years at most he will be missed from this home."

The public's concern about the future of this national treasure was answered. First by President Theodore Roosevelt, who established an Olympic National Monument in 1909, and later when the Congress and President Franklin Roosevelt established Olympic National Park in 1938.

Now, less than a century after the first explorers searched the Olympics and 50 years after the park was dedicated, it is in danger of being loved to death. Those who seek renewal and restoration through immersion in the wilderness must view the park's growing popularity with mixed feelings. In a complex, technical, and crowded world it is critical that we retain windows to the past so that each generation can see what this land was like before humans touched it.

Those of us who have experienced the Olympics have built a rich store of memories, rekindled every day we see their rugged outline etched in a western sunset sky. My personal love affair started in 1937 at Camp Parsons as a cub scout. A day hike up the Dosewallips was a tantalizing taste of what lay beyond. For 50 years, I have explored, climbed and traversed those mountains building vivid technicolor memories to carry me through drizzly gray winters and to inspire me for the next adventure.

I remember climbing toward Marmot Pass in December. The quiet swish of skis broke the deep silence of a world at sleep, while a glittering galaxy of stars cast soft shadows on the pristine powder.

I remember traversing the Olympic range from the Skokomish to the Hoh, retracing O'Neil's first trek. Elk looked on curiously as we trekked over ridges seldom visited. I felt kindred with the first explorers even though sixty years had passed since they had come this way. I remember plunging naked into scores of numbingly cold lakes and then warming myself in comfort on a glacially smooth rock drenched in sunshine. I remember stepping down from the ice and rock of Mount Olympus to the exquisite garden of the Queets Basin, isolated, alone and filled with the joy of a benign nature.

If these fifty years of wilderness experiences and of a national park are worth celebrating, it is even more important to learn how to preserve this wilderness experience for our children and theirs.

We must preserve the existing park and expand current boundaries whenever and wherever it is needed for appropriate protection.

We must manage to protect wilderness values first and accommodate visitor needs next.

We must ensure that we do not destroy the wilderness we seek to preserve by loving it to death through overuse.

While the fifty years of Olympic National Park have been years of extraordinary change and growth in the Northwest, they are only an instant in the creation of a unique wilderness.

The contributions which follow reflect the devotion and memory of just a few of the millions who have explored and experienced Olympic National Park. Savor each of them as you would the Olympics; carefully, completely and with affection.

— *Senator Daniel J. Evans*

Introduction

Less than one hundred years ago the first white explorers led parties to the uncharted interior of the Olympics to seek out the mysteries of this almost inaccessible corner of our country. The idea of a national park in the Olympics was first suggested in the 1890s by two of these early explorers, Lt. Joseph P. O'Neil and Judge James Wickersham. Many years passed after the first park proposal, but it was a dream that became a goal for many; and finally, with the merging of support by community leaders, conservationists from other areas, and the personal interest of President Franklin Roosevelt in 1937, the dream became a reality. Olympic National Park was established on June 29, 1938, after several decades of controversy and debate.

The story of the park is a classic example of the often seen struggle between conflicting values when lands are proposed for parks. The economic value of the heavily forested Olympic Peninsula is well known and, in the early years, offered the promise of an almost inexhaustible supply of high quality timber. This inevitably set up the struggle between those who focused on the long-term economic benefits and those who saw different, more intrinsic, values in the Olympics. Even those who thought both were possible wrestled with the question of how large the park should be. While this basic question was settled with the establishment of the park, philosophical skirmishes continued as the shape and size of the park changed over the years.

The rich combination of land forms, scenic beauty and abundant plant and animal life led to the realization that a national park, with few equals, had been created. The park now stretches from the rugged Washington coastline through the lush forests that line the dozen rivers whose sources are found high in the alpine meadows and glaciated peaks that form the heart of the Olympics.

Olympic National Park has joined a few very select national parks that have received worldwide recognition by being designated both an International Biosphere Reserve in 1976 and a World Heritage Site in 1981. Through these designations, the long-term value of Olympic, as a protected area, has been reinforced. It is now one of the world's important natural treasures and one of the most visited national parks in the United States.

The park's rich fabric provides a touchstone through which we can maintain contact with our natural world. There is little change here. The constancy of Olympic's ecosystems provides a foundation against which we measure the rapid change in the world around us. As this change continues at an increasing pace, places such as Olympic National Park are becoming biological islands. These places provide a vital link to keep us in tune with our natural heritage. For some, it is a place to touch nature and breathe in its restorative energy. For many it is an outdoor learning center. Others find it simply a magnificent outdoor playground. I often wonder if many of the visitors who come to the park think of those early park proponents who had the vision to know what this place could mean to us today. As the inheritors of this gift, we must be sure that the "public trust" that this national park represents is upheld, so that those who celebrate the next half century will feel even more strongly the responsibility to pass this park on unimpaired for future generations.

This anthology celebrates the fifty years of Olympic National Park. Its pages recall the history and feelings of those who brought it into being, the citizens who called for the establishment of the national park, and most importantly the people whose park it is to use and enjoy. It is this latter group which has provided most of the poems, stories, and historical accounts. This collection of writings presents a collage of experiences and emotions as diverse as the park itself.

This introduction would not be complete without recognizing the work of the wonderful *volunteer* committee that put this anthology together. They spent countless hours collecting, screening and assembling material. It seemed that everyone who was approached to contribute to the anthology gladly provided some of their writings. From the well-known authors to the local poets and writers, there was an outpouring of quality material to be considered. The work of the committee was a "labor of love" by people unified in their appreciation of the park. Their efforts produced a lasting gift for Olympic National Park's Golden Anniversary.

— Robert S. Chandler
Park Superintendent

SEASONS

THE PULSE OF THE SEASONS
by Robert L. Wood

Because the Olympic Peninsula lies at high latitude, closer to the North Pole than the Equator, the summer days are long, up to sixteen hours intervening between sunrise and sunset. During the warm months, from May through September, the trails become worn by the footfalls of the backpacker and the trailriders' horses. But to really know the Olympic Mountains one must visit them at all seasons because they have variable moods and present different faces as the seasons change with the turning of the earth. To see their sharp outlines softened by summer haze is not enough, for the peaks are equally interesting when shrouded in autumn's fogbanks and winter's mists, or in the spring, when they lurk behind dark clouds in an elusive game of hide-and-seek.

Snow usually begins to fall in the high country in October. The first autumn storm drenches the lowlands and whitens the higher summits and ridges left barren by the summer sun. This frosting of the mountaintops signals the approach of winter and indicates that hibernation time has arrived for the animals that sleep through cold months, and that migration time down to lower elevations has come for those who must face the winter awake. During this seasonal transition the weather pattern is variable and quick-changing. One day the skies are sunny, the air redolent with the mesmeric charm of Indian summer; the next, the sun has disappeared and ragged nimbus clouds scud across the skies, trailing rain as they move inland.

The dark days of November bring a chill to the land that replaces the transitory warmth of Indian summer. Gray clouds roll in relentlessly from the Pacific, releasing heavy rain on the lowlands. Higher up snow falls steadily and the snow line descends lower and lower on the mountainsides as the weather becomes colder. By the end of December the high country above four thousand feet lies deeply buried, and on clear days the mountains, snow-covered from base to summit, appear to have been chiseled from pure white marble. Now the peaks stand aloof, undisturbed by man except for a few hardy mountaineers.

Spring comes early to the lowlands, arriving in April when the dogwoods splash white against the conifers' somber greens, and climbs the mountainsides as the snowline recedes, to culminate at higher elevations when the rhododendron buds open in early July. Spring is uncertain and tentative in the Olympics, with damp, chilly weather, and fog lingering in the deep canyons. A noisy season, it contrasts vividly with the white silence of winter. The squawking of the ravens and the jays, and the booming of the streams carrying the melting snow to the sea are punctuated by the rumble of avalanches as tons of snow thunder down the mountainsides. On the lowlands the forest floor comes alive, exhibiting many shades of green, and the rain forests display their own special splendor.

In the high country spring fades almost imperceptibly into the brief but lovely summer. From early July until October the days are cool and sunny, warming in the afternoons. The morning skies are generally clear, but clouds often gather in the afternoon, when cumulus masses float around the higher peaks. Occasionally these develop into thunderheads accompanied by lightning and heavy showers, but this is rare. As night approaches the clouds dissipate, the air chills and the stars appear, incredibly bright in the blackness of the night sky.

Indian summer adds a delightful touch to the close of summer. The days are warm and pleasant, deceptive in that they give no hint of the approach of winter. Traveling is easiest then, for the high country trails are free of snow. In the lowland forests the maples turn scarlet and gold, accenting the dark green of the conifers, and the slim trunks of the alders stand starkly white beside the swift-flowing rivers. On high, exposed meadows above timberline huckleberry bushes glow like red and purple beacons, and the hiker is likely to see bears gorging on the berries to store fat for the coming winter hibernation. Nights become longer and crisper, frost comes to the higher elevations, and the stage is set for snowfall when autumn storms arrive. Once again ragged clouds move, wraithlike, across the timbered mountainsides and winter establishes itself among the high peaks, its cold, brooding stillness quietly and inexorably completing the majestic turn of the seasons.

Mt. Olympus

ANNIVERSARY

For Gunnar

We are at home among the old firs
on the Whiskey Bend Trail,
looking for the Press Party blazes,
ax-cuts that mark their way
to the illusionary warm springs
of the inner Olympics.
Our scars have healed like theirs,
on trees still standing,
bark converging on the wounds.

Through cottonwoods hazy with spring,
we look down from a rocky point
on old Anderson Ranch across the Elwha,
hear the river's roar
through the narrow walls of Goblin's Gate.
The muddy trail, slumped at the bench mark,
leads us down into the bleak beauty of a "silver forest,"
swept uphill by a blackening flash-fire
since we walked here last.
We straddle, like children in the afternoon,
downed logs over the trail above Geyser Valley,
stroke the rough satin bark
of the fallen wild cherry.

We are at home with fruitless old apple trees
at Cougar Mike's place;
countless suckers and brittle twigs
promise nothing;
at home with the slow streams
meandering soggy alder bottom,
where deers' white rumps
flash in sun as they enter the forest,
with flickers' grey backs among grey trunks.

The door is open at Humes Ranch
but not in welcome as it once was.
We look through web-netted windows
from the low kitchen where Lois stood, tall,
cooking and serving what Cris grew:
raspberries, picked under the screen
that kept out robins, and great kettles of spinach.

We sit on the sagging porch in late sun,
stare into the camera,
taking our own picture.
Our memories are like the drumming of the ruffed grouse,
muted and elusive,
mythical sounds of the inner springs.

— *Frances Fagerlund*

FOR THE BOY WHO WAS DODGER POINT LOOKOUT FIFTEEN YEARS AGO

[On a backpacking trip with my first wife in the Olympic mountains, having crossed over from the Dosewallips drainage, descended to and forded the Elwha and the Goldie, and climbed again to the high country. Hiking alone down the Elwha from Queets basin, these years later, brings it back.]

The thin blue smoke of our campfire
down in the grassy, flowery,
heather meadow
two miles from your perch.
The snowmelt pond, and Alison,
half-stoopt bathing like
Swan Maiden, lovely naked,
ringed with Alpine fir and
gleaming snowy peaks. We
had come miles without trails,
you had been long alone.
We talked for half an hour up
there above the foaming creeks
and forest valleys, in our
world of snow and flowers.

I don't know where she is now;
I never asked your name.
In this burning, muddy, lying,
blood-drenched world
that quiet meeting in the mountains
cool and gentle as the muzzles of
three elk, helps keep me sane.

—*Gary Snyder*

SUBALPINE AUTUMN
By Edward Tisch

Often, in early autumn, I'm near timberline finishing my last studies of the year. Through spring and summer I've worked my way upslope, trying to keep in step with the unfolding stages of plant growth. By late August the story is nearing completion. Down in the lowlands most species have flowered, set fruit, and begun to die back. This pattern holds true at middle elevations and, generally, in the high country. At upper levels, however, where open forest gives way to meadow, the arrival of autumn is not simply the end of summer, but a brilliant culmination where color streams from dying leaves and straggling flowers.

In the Olympics this is sometimes a crispy season. Subalpine environments take on a brittleness in autumn. The weather is crisp, as are the leaves underfoot, even the twigs on the trees. Temperatures frequently drop below freezing. The dew point is reached before suppertime, and morning frost coats vegetation well after sunrise, particularly on north slopes. The daily cycles of condensation, freezing and thaw purify the air. Everything smells clean. Certain conifers, notably subalpine fir and dwarf juniper, possibly Alaska cedar, fill the atmosphere with a unique pungence. Breathing deeply becomes a pleasure. I catch myself doing it again and again—like a boy re-experiencing some familiar childhood aroma.

Subalpine plants undergo pronounced physiologic reversals during their growing season. In April, May, and June, the period of vegetative emergence, most can tolerate considerable freezing. No matter how cold it gets they continue their upward expansion, some even pushing their way through little melt-holes in the snow. This is when underground food reserves move into plant growth areas, and low temperatures seem unable to reverse the upward flow. The leaves and stems continue their growth despite occasional frost. In late summer, however, as days progressively shorten, the freezing nights are more destructive. Now the food transfers are primarily downward into the roots and bulbs. When this occurs, the aerial plant parts begin to die back. I hesitate to call the reversal destructive, for it helps to accelerate the color changes so characteristic of autumn foliage.

In the Pacific Northwest we are blessed with the presence of several subalpine artists. I refer to a collection of timberline shrubs that have the capacity to put forth brilliant autumnal displays. While these plants grow relatively close to one another, their slightly differing ecologies result in unique juxtapositions of color.

The white rhododendron (*Rhododendron albiflorum*) is a three- to four-foot shrub that prefers forest but commonly skirts the edges of subalpine meadows. It forms golden hedges near the trunks and lower limbs of conifers, glowing brightly against the evergreen backdrop.

In among the rhododenrons we encounter two kinds of mountain-ash (*Sorbus scopulina* and *S. sitchensis*). These are somewhat taller, growing to six or eight feet, and have compound leaves that turn vivid orange or reddish-yellow. They also produce brilliant red berries that are taken by wildlife. Mountain-ash fruits remain essentially untouched through August and much of September, providing color long before the leaves change. These are generally the last berries to go. Animals avoid them as long as possible. Some folks suggest their flavor improves after frost.

The rhododendron borders are flanked by burgundy patches of mountain huckleberry *(Vaccinium membranaceum)*. While these rarely exceed three feet in height, their maroon leaves and tart berries make them a distinctive component of the forest-meadow ecotone. Historically, mountain huckleberries have been one of the mainstays of Northwest Indians, especially east of the Cascades.

Out a ways from the trees, where meadow species thrive, the taller shrubs are replaced by low-growing Cascade huckleberry *(V. deliciosum)*. This species turns bluish-purple in autumn and produces very tasty berries. It grows in close association with the white and pink heathers, so characteristic of our subalpine zone. Actually, by September heathers have shed their blossoms and look more like junipers than flowering plants.

This late in the season the mountain wildflowers are nearly gone. A few lupines continue to bloom near the tips of their stems, providing occasional patches of blue. We encounter bits of pink fireweed and scarlet Indian paintbrush. Here and there are nameless dots of yellow and a little white. The pearly everlasting is at its peak. But, generally speaking, our fall colors belong to the shrubs.

Subalpine autumn is of a transient nature. When night temperatures drop into the 20's, and snow mixes with the rain, the bright foliage soon disappears. The bittersweet combinations of frost, fresh air, dazzling color and, finally, leaf fall produce a sadly enchanting effect.

I sit on a log, lean against a scaly pine, and watch jays and nutcrackers pick at maturing cones. Pieces of seed trickle through the branches and gather in the drying grass. The jay voices are harsh—almost rusty and metallic. When the birds take off they glide noisily over and between the treetops. A few juncos scratch near the path, then bounce away, flicking their tails.

Some of the leaves are beginning to fade now. A few have already fallen. They do this so quietly, barely rustling in their descent. There's a distant hissing sound in the air—maybe a breeze in the treetops—or westerlies bringing storms from the coast. Banks of cloud are gathering above the Bailey Range. It's distinctly cooler.

I take a few deep breaths, gaze wistfully across the mountains, then rise and set out for home — back to the lowlands. I keep looking over my shoulder.

Pasque flowers

POLE OF REMOTENESS
by Harvey Manning

The plan was to sit tight in Seattle until the onset of the Midwinter Clear, a meteorological phenomenon the wise men said was an invariable annual event, occurring sometime between Santa Claus and the Easter Bunny. By so waiting we would avoid the fate of the many groups of our friends who had set off on fixed dates and spent days floundering in rain-forest rain, dodging widow-makers and flying moss. I always greeted them cheerfully when they returned, wrinkled up like prunes, and was full of smart remarks, since nothing in my life plan was more certain than that I never would attempt the first winter ascent of Mount Olympus.

Eventually I did sign on for a trip, as a favor to a friend who needed a third person to meet a Park Service requirement. I rested easy, long since having wised up about Santa Claus and the Easter Bunny and the Midwinter Clear. Nobody ever went broke betting against good weather on Olympus, winter *or* summer.

Well, subsequently I took to hanging my Christmas stocking with care and putting out a bunch of carrots Easter eve, because *the Clear came.*

I should explain that in the period of these events I was rapidly reverting to my natural condition of valley-pounder and ridge-runner, increasingly hostile to any peak that demanded I soil my hands on it. However, I continued to be a devout "semiexpeditioner," meaning I understood why Mallory and Smythe and Shipton did what they did, but I wasn't English and thus couldn't go to Everest and so did what was possible locally, on short time and short cash, to escape. The "Washington pole of remoteness"—the spot in the state the farthest from downtown Seattle—fascinated me the way the South Pole did Robert Falcon Scott. Queets Basin, Luna Cirque, they were my sort of place.

I knew, of course, the *true* pole of remoteness was somewhere in winter, when wilderness expands by several orders of magnitude. The reason I didn't do much winter mountaineering was snow. In summer, in amounts proportionate to other elements of the landscape, it's exceedingly picturesque and excellent for cold drinks. In winter, however, it gets completely out of hand.

Part of my distaste was due to the primitive condition of our technology, which hadn't advanced very far beyond inventing the wheel. In winter you had to be busy, busy, busy all the time, less in hopes of ever getting really comfortable than to avoid freezing to death. Vilhjalmur Stefansson, who stuck it to the Englishmen (whose polar expeditions always ended in disaster) by writing a book called *The Friendly Arctic*, said, "An adventure is a sign of incompetence." The wilderness is more exciting if you don't know too much or own too much. Well, there are other things in life besides excitement.

Monday night, January 29, we drove from Seattle to the end of the Hoh River road, arriving after midnight. The ranger, bless his heart, got up to greet us and let us sleep in the bunkhouse—unheated. I thought the thermometer on the wall must be broken and wondered if it was the chattering of my teeth that did it.

I have to admit that Tuesday was a champion of a day, the Clear gleaming blue through the giant trees, bands of elk tromping and chomping around in the snow. The temperature was twenty degrees—in the sun, when it managed to push a ray through the cathedral roof. It wasn't a whole lot warmer inside our Khaki Gang costumes of Army packs, Army parkas, Army boots, Army mittens and socks and long-handled underwear. We had Army feather bags so we wouldn't necessarily die in our sleep, but a breather on the trail was risky—you could feel your blood sludging and brain turning silly. The good thing was that we were able to carry the Army beavertails on our backs and walk the whole fifteen valley miles on a rain crust solid as concrete. At dusk we reached the Elk Lake shelter, where some saint had left a stack of dry wood that let us get as deliriously warm as Sam McGee at his cremation.

Wednesday we started up the slope, ran out of rain crust and put on snowshoes, and soon took them off as the angle steepened. On a route that in summer is an easy trail, we roped up, chopped steps in icicles, and belayed over avalanche chutes, too busy to pay much attention to the gray sheet sliding across the sky from the south. So much for the Clear.

At Glacier Meadows we glissaded down a snow wall into an icebox— a brand-new lean-to shelter—and shoveled and stomped and scraped most of the afternoon, trying to bring the accommodations up to the minimum for survival. When we'd done everything possible, we had an hour left

Blue Glacier—Mt. Olympus

before the end of the world and snowshoed through frosted Christmas trees in snow as airy as talcum powder to the edge of the Blue Glacier.

The glacier *was* blue in the twilight, and so were the glazed cliffs and the icefall, and the clouds rushing north a mile a minute, beheading the peaks of Olympus and lowering onto the Snow Dome. Even the wind felt blue.

I had recently seen *Scott of the Antarctic,* the greatest expedition film ever made, and in this gale on Olympus could hear the gale over the South Pole—and Vaughan Williams' music—and the words Scott had written in his journal on January 17, forty-one years earlier: "The Pole...Great God! This is an awful place..."

Snow began blasting from the Pole. We snowshoed back to the lean-to and slid down in our hole and managed to set frozen squaw wood to smoldering enough to strangle and blind us and eventually to cook what Scott would have called "a fat Polar hoosh in spite of our chagrin"—chicken noodle soup and corned beef, with chunks of pumpernickel and butter. A restaurant that could duplicate the dish would make a fortune. If it could draw enough customers to such a place. Because the place was the secret ingredient, of course.

Thursday morning we banqueted on a pot of oatmeal and prunes and Eagle Brand condensed sweetened milk. With the wheezing and the weeping, that occupied the morning. At noon we opened khaki tins of Army miscalled pemmican and drank cocoa with marshmallows and Eagle Brand. I decided that if I somehow ever had to go hiking in winter again I'd make darned sure to take plenty of Eagle Brand.

Combined with the smoke it impelled us out into the blizzard—not to attempt an ascent, purely for the exercise—and onto the Blue Glacier—blue no more—pure white underfoot and overhead and all around. We couldn't see each other, only the rope stretching off the white void.

Why were we here?

On the last January 17 of his life Scott wrote in his journal, "Well, it is something to have got here..."

The gale roared on, and I wondered if the avalanche chutes on the trail were roaring yet. Until we crossed them and descended to the big trees it was a waste to discuss what-all we'd put on our hamburgers in Queets, how many pitchers of beer we'd drink in Seattle. Olympus wasn't in the same space-time as Seattle. Or Queets. Or the nice ranger at the end of the Hoh road. It was as far away as I'd ever been, and probably farther than I had any need to be.

Thursday night there was more smoke and hoosh and blizzard. It was a happy little hole in the snow, but not so happy we didn't have a few thoughts about home. The soonest we could be there, with luck, was Saturday or Sunday. The ranger, and our support party in Seattle, had been told not to worry until Wednesday or Thursday or so. That didn't mean we couldn't, a little.

ORIGINS

OROGRAPHY

An ocean of air
Washes over these mountains
Water falls everywhere.

— *Jeremy Anderson*

THE ORIGIN OF LAKE CRESCENT

Lake Crescent lies on the north side of the Olympic Peninsula, not far from the Strait of Juan de Fuca. The highest mountain overlooking it is Mount Storm King.

Many, many years ago, the Klallam people and the Quileute people had a big battle near the shores of the Strait of Juan de Fuca. For two days they fought, from sunrise to sunset. Many warriors on both sides were killed, but neither side would ask for peace.

After watching the bloodshed for two long days, Mount Storm King became angry. On the third day he broke off a great piece of rock from his head and hurled it down into the valley. The rock was so huge that it killed all the men fighting in the valley below him, all the Klallam warriors and all the Quileute.

Through the valley flowed a small river. The rock hurled by Mount Storm King dammed up this stream, and soon at the foot of the mountain where the fighting had been fiercest a peaceful little lake sparkled in the sunshine. For many generations no Indian ever went to the place where the warriors had been punished by death.

The little lake is still there—Lake Crescent it is called today. And Mount Storm King, mirrored in its clear depths, still looks out across the Strait of Juan de Fuca and over the forest-covered mountains on both sides of it. Storm King guards the crescent-shaped shore line and the calm blue waters of the lake he made long ago.

—Makah legend

TALE OF THE RIDGEPOLE
As Told by the Carver, David //// (Forlines)

Once long ago there was an old man who was the last head whaler of the coastal people. When his hair turned white, he had his first and only son to inherit his whaling position in the tribe.

When his son turned twelve years old, the old man got a crew together to go whaling. He told his village that he was going to take his son to teach him before the old one died. The village was against the old man taking this very young boy out to sea.

Early in the morning, the crew started out to sea with the old one and his son in the bow under the cover. It is said that if the whale sees the one who is to take its life, the whale will make it storm and kill all.

Under the cover, the old one was praying and talking to his son, "When it comes time to spear the whale, you step back out of the way, my son." The old one told the crew which way to turn and where the whale was going to come up.

When the whale came up alongside, the boy stepped back and the old man speared it. The harpoon hit the whale and the boy was pulled over the side as the rope played out, for the boy had stepped into the coils of the rope.

The crew managed to get a couple of sealskin floats attached to the rope and just hang on, hoping the boy would break free. It seemed as if a long time passed and the boy never came up anywhere.

The whale finally stopped pulling and the crew looked everywhere for the boy. The old man was totally heartbroken and realized the people were wiser than he. As they turned for home, one float, then the other, surfaced.

There was the boy with blood coming from his ears, eyes, mouth and nose as he floated on the surface. The crew quickly retrieved the boy. Placing him in his father's arms, they returned to their village.

The people were very angry at the old one for taking his son to sea at such a young age. Four days and nights passed with the boy still unconscious. Then he came straight up out of bed singing one of the most beautiful songs the people had ever heard. After the song the boy told the people how he had been able to stay alive under water so long.

The boy said that when the rope around his legs pulled him into the water, he knew he was going with the whale. The whale began talking to the boy: "Crawl down the rope to me," it said. "As I did and got into a bubble of air by his blow-hole, the whale began singing a very beautiful song. I just hung on till the song ended with the whale's life. It was very dark and cold when I started up. My head pounded and as I floated up the water was in layers. Each layer was a different color and had a song to go with it. Each song was more beautiful than the last. I went to sleep on the surface."

Four months later, the boy took a crew and went whaling. At the age of 12, he brought back the largest whale ever seen and became the head whaler of his people as his fathers before him.

POEM FOR THE NAMING OF
THE CLEARING ABOVE SHI SHI
"NEVER-LOOK-BACK"
(July 12, 1971)

for John Utti

Climbing the trail up from
    Portage head,
Wet with morning rain,
    foot slipping...
How many have reached for
      this same branch!

— *Robert Sund*

HO, HŌ, HOH

Star husbands,
the ones the women liked to think of,
shinnied down ropes and dropped to the floor
of soft selagenella and feathermoss.
The little red one, the big bright one,
became Wapiti

the Elk-people,
the weather-satellites of the Hoh.
Every step they took
parallel the crashing mountain creeks
the upward-spiralling force of the Earth
with
the downward-spiralling force of heaven:
the Elk-people
pass by a huge piece of granite erratic
on the Rainforest path
once every hundred years
they rub their silken muzzles
against the boulder

and when the stone is finally rubbed to nothingness
in this manner
as much time will have passed
as if you used the Mind
alone
to attain the Way.

> —*R. T. Landry*
> from "Ho, Hō, Hoh,
> a Mythos of the Hoh River"

Ho is Chinese for 'river'
Hō is Japanese for 'Dharma'
Hoh is Ohalet for 'fast moving water'

THUNDERBIRD AND WHALE

These two legends come from the Quileute. The first was related by Jack Ward of La Push, Washington; he had learned it from his father, who died in 1945 at the age of about 98. The second is blending of a fragment told by two good informants, one of whom explained that Thunderbird represented good and Killer Whale represented evil.

Long ago, as long as two men can live, there was a sad time in the land of the Quileute. For days and days great storms blew. Rain and hail and then sleet and snow came down upon the land. The hailstones were so large that many of the people were killed. The other Quileute were driven from their coast villages to the great prairie, which was the highest part of their land.

There the people grew thin and weak from hunger. The hailstones had beaten down the ferns and the camas and the berries. Ice locked the rivers so that the men could not fish. Storms rocked the ocean so that fishermen could not go out in their canoes for deep-sea fishing. Soon the people had eaten all the grass and roots on the prairie. There was no food left. As babies and children died without food, even the strongest and bravest of their fathers could do nothing. They had called upon the Great Spirit for help, but no help had come.

At last the great chief of the Quileute called a meeting of his people. He was old and wise. In his youth he had been the bravest of the warriors, the swiftest of the runners, the fiercest of a fierce tribe.

"Take comfort, my people," said the great chief to his people. "We will call again upon the Great Spirit for help. If no help comes, then we will know that it is His will that we die. If it is not His will that we live, then we will die bravely, as brave Quileute have always died. Let us talk with the Great Spirit."

So the weak and hungry people sat in silence while the chief talked with the Great Spirit who had looked kindly upon the Quileute for hundreds and hundreds of years.

When his prayer had ended, the chief turned again to his people. "Now we will wait for the will of the One who is wise and all-powerful."

The people waited. No one spoke. There was nothing but silence and darkness. Soon there came a great noise, and flashes of lightning cut the darkness. Then the people heard another noise. A deep, whirring sound, as the beat of giant wings, came from the place of the setting sun. All the people turned their eyes toward the sky above the ocean as a huge, bird-shaped creature flew toward them.

This bird was larger than any they had ever seen. Its wings, from tip to tip, were twice as long as a war canoe. It had a huge, curving beak, and its eyes glowed like fire. The people saw that its great claws held a giant whale—a living, giant whale.

In silence they watched while Thunderbird—for so the bird was named by everyone—carefully lowered the whale to the ground before them. Thunderbird then flew high into the sky, gave one earth-reaching cry, and went back to the thunder and lightning it had come from. Perhaps it flew back to its perch in the hunting grounds of the Great Spirit.

Thunderbird and Whale saved the Quileute from dying. The people knew that the Great Spirit had heard their prayer. Even today they never forget that visit of Thunderbird, never forget that it ended long days of hunger and death. For on the prairie near their village are big, round stones that the old grandfathers say are the hardened hailstones of that storm of long ago.

2

Thunderbird is a very large bird, with feathers as long as a canoe paddle. When he flaps his wings, he makes the thunder and the great winds. When he opens and shuts his eyes, he makes the lightning. In stormy weather, he flies through the skies, flapping his wings and opening and closing his eyes.

Thunderbird's home is a cave in the Olympic Mountains, and he wants no one to come near it. If hunters get so close that he can smell them, he makes the thunder noise, and he rolls ice out of his cave. The ice rolls down the mountainside, and when it reaches a rocky place it breaks into many, many pieces. The pieces rattle as they roll farther down into the valley.

All the hunters are so afraid of Thunderbird and his noise and his rolling ice that they never stay long near his home. No one ever sleeps near his cave.

SOLEDUCK IN JULY

Down at the riffle they're
delicate as gnat-wings,
gangly as polliwogs and cranes.

The women wading discover hot mud.
Its sweet gush between toes
squinches their ecstatic eyes shut.

— *Bill Ransom*

THE BLUEJAY

Many Indian people say that a long time ago, animals and people lived as brothers. They tried to get along and help each other as best they could. In one part of our land there was a place with no daylight. It was always dark. Day after day, moon after moon, winter after winter, always there was darkness. The daylight was hidden away in the heart of the forest. It was kept in a small shed. This shed had a door which opened and slammed shut once every few seconds. Inside the shed, on one of the walls, hung a bag. In the bag was the sunlight. Also inside the shed were fierce animals who guarded the daylight. They wanted to keep it always for themselves. They would attack anyone who dared to enter their door.

In the same dark land lived the Bluejay. He was a tall, proud fellow who thought himself very important. He liked to tell about wonderful things that he would do someday. The Bluejay was tired of always having darkness. One day he decided that he must be the one to rescue daylight and give it back to his people. Wasn't he able to fly swiftly and wasn't he very clever? He thought. "I, my fellow tribesmen, shall go into the forest and get the daylight for you," he announced. "Oh no," cried the animals and people. "You must not go!" They all said, "You will be killed!" They knew that if the Bluejay went into the deep forest after the daylight, they would never see him again. Many others, who were stronger and smarter had gone to rescue the daylight and they had never been heard from again. The Bluejay's little sister cried loudest of all, "Please, my brother, do not do this foolish thing!" But it was no use. The Bluejay had made up his mind.

The next day dawned dark and black as usual. The Bluejay started out for the shed in the deep forest. A few of the braver members of the tribe had decided to go with him so he would not be alone in his last hours. In the light from their fire torches, they left the saddened village and made their way into the deep woods. All too soon they came to the little shed in the forest where daylight was kept. Right away the Bluejay began to plan how he would make his daring rescue. He watched the door carefully. 'Open— then shut.' He saw how the bag hung on the wall. 'Open—then shut.' He saw how far the wall was from the door. 'Open—then shut.' He thought how fast he would have to fly to reach the bag, hung on the wall, and then fly back out the door. 'Open—then shut.' His plan had to be perfect. He could not make a mistake.

Finally, the time was right. Muscles tense, head bent forward, eyes watching sharply, the Bluejay was ready to dart through the door the moment it swung open. 'Open! Shut! Open! Shut! Now!' With the speed of lightning, the Bluejay darted in past the startled animals and grabbed the bag from the wall! 'Swish!' He was almost all the way out of the door when, Slam! The door had closed on the back of his head. During the struggle, the bag of daylight had fallen to the ground and was spilling slowly over the entire land. As the tribesmen saw the daylight and felt its warmth, they began to shout with joy!

A great potlatch was held in honor of the Bluejay. Dancing and feasting lasted for days and days. Daylight had come to the dark land and all was gladness now. At last Bluejay had done something he could really be proud of! As for Bluejay's poor head, which had been caught in the slamming door, it now had a little peak on the back of it. And that is the way it is to this very day.

Source unknown
Submitted by Jamie R. Valadez, Klallam

A TALE OF TWO SEAS
by Tim McNulty

"A splendid confusion" were the words Captain Charles Barnes chose to describe the interior Olympics when he first viewed them from a ridgetop near Mount Wilder in 1890. And they remained a splendid confusion for geologists until quite recently. Only with the development of plate tectonics theory have the varied and sometimes contradictory pieces of the Olympics' geological origins begun to fall into place. We now know that the Olympic Peninsula was formed beneath the sea, carried in, and grafted onto the continent of North America.

The story begins when the area that is now the Olympic Peninsula was covered by a sea. It proceeds through fifty-five million years of sedimentary accumulations, suboceanic lava flows, sandstone slurries flowing out onto deep ocean floors, and the slow fine drift of silt through ages of calm coastal waters. It tells of intense pressure beneath the weight of millions of years of accumulated sediments, and of the slow but relentless collision of the ocean floor and the North American continent.

As mountains go, the Olympics are a fairly recent range, possibly as young as ten to twelve million years, and made up of relatively young rocks. The erosive forces that worked them into their present shape are very much alive today. A slight climatic shift, a drop of a few degrees in the mean annual temperature can cause, as it has in the not-too-distant past, dramatic transformations of the earth. Those forces—the tremendous erosive powers of glaciers and moving water and the quarrying strength of the rock and silt they carry, the incremental shaping of wind and frost action and the chemical weathering of soil—have combined to give us in the Olympics a landscape of breathtaking beauty and grace. It is the beauty of the earth unaltered by the hand of man. But altered it has been—altered and shaped exquisitely by another hand, whose fingers are of mists and rain, whose wrist is the eternal gesture of wind, and from whose palm flow the rivers which carry grains of feldspar, mica, and quartz from one range of mountains, still lifting, to the next, just beginning to form on the outwash plains and ocean floors—the slopes and summits of a future age.

On a clear, crisp morning from the summit of Mount Olympus, in the wilderness heart of the park, surrounded by a sea of snow-capped ridges and peaks, one can look out to the distant hazy blue of the Pacific. Perhaps a cool steady wind is blowing out of the southwest, and as the morning lengthens, a few clouds may gather along the ridgecrests. As we look from the distant waves of the sea to the slower, more pronounced earth waves that we know as mountains, we may feel that the two have more in common than shape and motion, more than the obvious exchange of wind and weather.

By looking with the eyes of a geologist, one might discern, far beneath the curved blue plane of the Pacific and its floor, another larger and infinitely more powerful sea. Geologists now generally believe that the continents and ocean floors are made up of vast segments of the earth's crust called plates. These plates float on a sea of semiliquid, intensely heated rock, which is the earth's mantle. It is believed that this lower sea flows in slow-moving convection currents, which cause drifting plates to collide with one another. It was one such collision, occuring in starts and pauses over a thirty-million-year period, that gave birth to the Olympic Mountains. In the area that is now the Olympics, the ocean floor and the North American continent were drifting irrevocably toward each other. Something had to give.

Point of the Arches

Normally where oceans and continents collide, ocean floors dip beneath the continents in a process called subduction, and continents override the ocean floors. In the area that was to become the Olympics the process was complicated by several factors, one of which—the formation of a suboceanic mountain range—was the result of molten lava flowing through large fissures in the ocean floor just off the coast. About thirty million years ago, this range began to be rafted toward the continent by the landward movement of the ocean floor. As the ocean floor dipped below the continent, the volcanic range, along with some of its associated sediments, was too much for the subduction process to follow. As a result of this and other factors, these volcanic basalts and sediments were scraped off the ocean floor and plastered onto the continent's edge. As the process continued, additional sediments accumulated on the ocean side of this volcanic rock. Then the incredibly powerful tectonic forces had their way with the amassed rock, bending, warping, faulting, and deforming it, remorselessly mixing the pieces of the puzzle.

Also during this period the subduction process slowed enough to allow the relatively lighter, less dense sedimentary and volcanic rocks to "float" upward, forming a high mountainous mass or dome. In turn, this mountain uplift initiated a cycle of erosion by wind, water, and ice, which over millions of years and at least six separate Ice Age advances has shaped the serrated ridges and peaks and the deep valley canyons that give the Olympics their present face. Today the undersea volcanic rocks are represented by the Crescent formation, whose tough basalt bedrock is found in the high summits of Mount Storm King and Mount Angeles along the northern edge of the park, and in the Needles and Mount Constance along the park's east side. Most of the rocks of the interior Olympics, such as Mount Anderson and Mount Olympus, are formed of sediments—largely sand and mud—that were deposited on the ocean side of the volcanic undersea range.

Darkness approached slowly, as it does on late summer evenings in the mountains. I was dropping back down the smooth sloping shoulder of Del Monte Ridge to Constance Pass in the eastern Olympics. My camp was on a shelf above Home Lake on the Dungeness side of the pass, and as usual I had ambled off farther than remaining daylight made prudent. As I reached the pass, the last light rippled hazily off Gray Wolf Ridge to the north, and the sky was lit with a soft, muted rose. Already the deep shadows of the valley were climbing the talus slopes and steep, textured walls of Inner Constance and Warrior Peak. The upper snowfields had caught the rose light of the sky and held it. The mountain wilderness, still as breath, had once more penetrated that elaborate construct we make of ourselves in the world, and left me with an all-pervasive sense of happiness and well-being.

HOW KWATEE MADE THE RIVERS AND ROCKS

Chief Wolf looked around on the beach early in the morning. He wanted to get anything that was washed in. Chief Wolf sometimes murdered people. When Kwatee learned about the murders, he decided to do something. He put up a cabin near the beach. Under the cabin he dug a well. He planned to murder Chief Wolf.

Later, Chief Wolf had a surf duck for Kwatee. "Here's a surf duck for you," he said.

"I'm sick," answered Kwatee. "I can't go out of my house. Will you stay with me tonight?"

Chief Wolf stayed that night. Kwatee made a big fire. When Chief Wolf was snoring, Kwatee took his knife and killed him. He put Chief Wolf's head in the well under the cabin and buried it.

Chief Wolf's family came to look for him. "He passed by late in the evening." Kwatee told them. "Come in. I'll find where he is through my spiritual."

Kwatee sang a song. "Leave the door open wide," he sang. "Leave the door open wide. Stand back, so that there is open space before the door."

Kwatee had his comb and his vessel of hair oil hanging in the doorway.

He sang his song again. In this song he admitted that he had murdered Chief Wolf. Then he ran away. He seized his comb and his hair oil and ran.

The Wolf family followed him. When the Wolf in front reached to grab him, Kwatee stuck his comb in the sand. The teeth became the hills and rocks on the point. Then Kwatee ran down the coast. When the Wolf family came close, he poured hair oil on the beach and made a river. And with the teeth of his comb he made rocks along the shore. That is how he made the Quillayute River and the Hoh, the Queets River and the Quinault—all the rivers along the coast, from Neah Bay down to the Columbia. And he made all the rocky points with his comb.

When he got out his canoe, Kwatee sang a song about a man-eating shark. He would kill the man-eating shark out in the ocean, he sang. But the man-eating shark swallowed Kwatee and his canoe. From inside its stomach, Kwatee killed the man-eating shark. Its dead body was washed in on the shore.

Early in the morning a man saw a shark had been washed in. He called to the others, and they planned to cut it up for food, after breakfast. When they started to cut it, Kwatee hollered from inside the shark, "Be careful. Don't cut me."

"What is that?" the men asked. "Someone is inside his stomach."

They cut a hole in the stomach of the shark and Kwatee ran out. He ran into his house. The people hollered at him, "That's Kwatee! That's Kwatee!"

—Quinault legend

PLACE NAMES OF OLYMPIC NATIONAL PARK
by Smitty Parratt

Glacier-clad mountains tower above deep rain forest valleys. Rivers flow from these verdant valleys into the sea along 58 miles of wild coastline. Within these nearly one million acres which comprise Olympic National Park, humans have named over 600 hundred places. Each name has a story. Collectively these stories are vignettes into the history of the Olympics.

Many of the geographic names are very logical. They are based on obvious facts or the nature of the place. Low Divide, at the head of the North Fork Quinault and Elwha valleys, is the lowest passage through the central Olympics, at only 3,650 feet. The pass was used by the Seattle Press Expedition during the winter of 1889-1890. They became the first to cross the inner Olympics and make such a detailed geographic report.

High Divide, at 5,000 feet elevation, between the Soleduck and Hoh valleys, provides unsurpassed vistas of Mt. Olympus and the Blue Glacier. Snow Dome, on the Blue Glacier, is a rounded mass of snow and ice. Hole-in-the-Wall is a rock arch 1 and 1/2-miles north of Rialto Beach which a person can walk through. Father and Son is a formation further north along the Pacific Coast, two rocks which resemble a father and son out for a walk, as viewed from the beach. The High-Hoh bridge is located 150 feet above the Hoh River.

Some areas may not be so obvious at first, but upon closer examination still make sense. Sundown Lake, at the head of Graves Creek above the Quinault Valley, is hemmed in by mountains. There is an opening only to the west, where the sun can shine through at sunset, illuminating the mountain walls at sundown.

A number of locations in the park honor plants and animals. Cedar Lake off of the Upper Gray Wolf Valley is surrounded by yellow cedar trees. Lone Tree, along the Bailey Range, is a mountain hemlock tree which makes a popular campsite along the open ridgetop.

The river valley Elwha is a Klallam Indian word which means "elk," reminding us of the herds of elk which still inhabit the valley today. Gray Wolf River is said to honor the last wolf in the Olympics, killed by A. B. Cameron, in the 1930's. Salmon Cascades, along the Soleduck River, makes highly visible the attempts of salmon to return to their birthplaces.

The geology and topography of the Olympics are fascinating and diverse. Pyrites Creek, which flows into the Quinault River, has deposits of iron pyrite, or "fools gold," along its course. Thousand Acre Meadow, named by Lloyd Hunt in 1932, is the largest unbroken subalpine meadow in the park, and is actually about 400 acres. On your first glance into Seven Lakes Basin from High Divide, you may think something is wrong, for there are far more than seven lakes. There is even Lake No. Eight, but the joke stops there, with the other ponds going unnamed.

Irely Lake, in the North Fork Quinault rain forest, recalls Jacob Irely, who while burning brush on his homestead backyard in 1891, caused a 3000 acre fire, the "Quinault Burn." Dodwell-Rixon Pass, at the headwaters of the Elwha River, is named for Arthur Dodwell and Theodore Rixon, who surveyed the forests of the Olympic Peninsula in 1899-1900.

One day in 1899, Caroline Jones was chopping wood in the back yard of her "Fairholme," when Theodore Rixon, surveyor, walked by. He noticed her efforts, offered to help, and they became enamored of one another. He honored his beloved by naming the last major unnamed Olympic peak for her, Mt. Carrie. Mt. Childs honors George Washington Childs, owner of the Philadelphia Ledger. During and following the Seattle Press Expedition of 1889-1890 several newspaper owners, including Childers, were honored with place names since the expedition was funded by a newspaper.

The first human inhabitants of the Olympic Peninsula were Native Americans. They too had names for places. Many of these have survived, although somewhat metamorphosed. Of 13 major rivers draining the Olympic Peninsula, all but one presently carry names derived from Native American names. Only the Dungeness River, named by Captain George Vancouver in 1792 for resemblance to the Dungeness area of his English homeland, is not of Indian origin. Hoh, for example, is said to mean "fast white water," while the translation for Ozette is not known. Bogachiel means "gets riley (muddy) after a rain," and Soleduck, "sparkling water."

In Queets Indian history, Kwatee the Creator was walking up the ocean beach once and came upon what is called the Queets River. No humans existed then. He waded the river, than sat down on the other side to rub the circulation back into his legs. Little balls of dirt formed under his hands; he threw two into the river and caused to come forth from them the first two humans. He called the couple "k witz qu," "people who come from the dirt of the skin," and this legend is the source of the "Queets River."

In the old days, Indians would pole their cedar dugout canoes up rivers in the fall to acquire elk, salmon, and berries for winter food. One such fall, up the Queets, a "klooch," or woman, wandered off to pick berries. She did not return. A major storm descended; the rest looked high and low for her, but could not find her. Finally they lifted their eyes high and saw her atop a high ridge. She had climbed there and wrapped her blanket around her, looking for them from the vantage point, but she had frozen to death. She is still visible there today as Kloochman Rock, standing sentinel on the ridge.

What do Olympic National Park place names tell us? They speak of natural features, personal impressions, plants, animals, funny and tragic happenings. They share geology, pioneer history, Indian history, and mythology. They add a dimension of human interest to the backcountry. Without these names, the places would speak for themselves with their wild beauty. But the names are with us, and the natural character of these places, intertwined with the human side in place names, weaves a rich tapestry, the continuing story of people experiencing the wild Olympics.

Lake Crescent

EXPLORATIONS

BOGACHIEL RIVER

In raingear
way too big, you
stupid kid run
knee-deep
through the creek
and laugh. "I like
to get my feet wet!"
Your face grins
snot down your lip.
"You're gonna," I say
"get cold—got
4 more miles to walk."
And you shout, "Look
Daddy, my feet
clean outa sight!"

A mile
up-trail we stop
under spruce,
take off socks
and shoes, thaw
your shriveled feet
on my stomach.
You whimper. Rain
drips through sky
and limbs—these
damn November days,
dark before we
reach the shelter.
We fooled around
too long, skipping
rocks, watching Coho
spawning in the river.
I was afraid of that.

Mosquito Creek
we take out flashlights.
"Daddy watch this!"
Your light bounces
black soaked trees.
You laugh. I
catch my breath.
I'm beat tired
lagging
on your heels—
still 2 1/2 miles
to go. It would
have got dark
before the shelter,
even if we'd
hurried, even
if you'd had no fun.

— *Kenyon Nattinger*

BREAKING NEW GROUND
by Gifford Pinchot

My next job was to have a look at the Olympic Reserve, also in the State of Washington, which rejoices in the heaviest rainfall in the United States. I suppose there is nowhere, except in the Redwood belt of California, a more magnificent body of woodland. From Lake Crescent with Al Blackwood, a first-class woodsman, I made a trip to see the supermagnificent forest on Section 16, Township 30, Range 9 West. So thick was the undergrowth, so formidable the down timber, and so dense the forest, that it took us from ten in the morning until seven in the evening to make less than five miles.

And no wonder. Many of the trees were 275 feet in height, and not a few of them were 10 or 12 feet through breast high, or even more. Douglas fir, Western cedar, Sitka spruce, and Western hemlock were the principal kinds. The Douglas fir, which made up nearly half the forest, would average 200 feet high and 6 feet in diameter, with 100 feet of clear trunk. Near a settler's cabin I measured a fir foot log across a stream. It was 134 feet long, 26 inches through the butt, and 18 inches at the top. In 134 feet it had lost only 8 inches in diameter.

The overpowering sense of bigness which emanated from that gigantic forest I can never forget. One of the photographs I took of it, duly enlarged, hung on my wall for years. I saw it many times a day, and always with wonder and delight. A windfall in timber like that was something to work through.

But the most significant thing I found, and to me it was an amazing discovery, was that every part of the Reserve I saw appeared to have been cleared by fire within the last few centuries. The mineral soil under the humus, wherever it was exposed about the roots of windfalls, was overlaid by a layer of charcoal and ashes. Continuous stretches of miles without a break were covered with a uniform growth of Douglas fir from two to five feet in diameter, entirely unscarred by fire. Among them numerous rotting stumps of much larger trees did bear the marks of burning. "I did not see a single young seedling of Douglas fir under the forest cover, nor a single opening made by fire which did not contain them."

Fires conditioned and controlled the forest in the Olympics. Fires burned not only in the summer, but, believe it or not, in the rain-soaked winter also. They burned far down into the deep layer of humus, and into fallen logs, especially hemlock logs, and often survived the pouring rains. I was told that on the trail from Wineton to Beaver a fire which began in August 1896, survived the winter in this way, and was still burning in February 1897.

Next to fire, the thing that surprised me most was the incredible reproduction of the Western hemlock. Its seedlings stood in crowded rows on nearly every fallen log. Others sent their rootlets down from the tops of broken stubs, over the rotting wood to the wood to the humus and mineral soil sometimes twenty or thirty feet beneath. When their supports disintegrate, the young hemlocks are left to stand on their leg-like roots, propped high above the ground, until at length the separate roots unite into a single stem. To all appearances it is like an ordinary tree trunk grown up from the ground instead of down from the sky, except that it is a little thicker and less regular near the base.

At Lake Crescent, to my great delight, Dr. C. Hart Merriam turned up, and we went together by way of Soleduck Hot Springs to the Hoh River Divide, from which the view of Mt. Olympus was beyond description. I never saw the classical original, but if the gods of ancient Greece had anything approaching this peak to live on, they were certainly in luck.

From this camp Blackwood and I went on foot down the Bogachiel River. It was a great trip. I believed then, and I may have been right, that white men had never passed that way before. At any rate, for three days we saw no trace of humans, but only wolf tracks and the deep-worn trails of the Olympic elk.

Although it was only the end of August, one night it rained so hard that Blackwood and I had to pile our fire of driftwood high and wide to keep it from being drowned out, while we sat in our leaky brushwood lean-to, hoping against hope that the heat would dry us faster than the rain could wet us down. I tell you again, them was the happy days.

Finally, through the settled portions of the Soleduck Valley to the little settlement of Sappho, from which, just the week before, a mountain lion had carried off a child. It was the only case I ever knew of, outside the nature fakers, and on the very spot it was extremely real.

THE EARLY EXPLORATION OF
THE OLYMPIC PENINSULA
by Robert L. Wood

Pioneers in the Pacific Northwest found the Olympic Peninsula a strange, wild land. Nature was prolific on a grand scale, and the vast resources, seemingly impossible of exhaustion, were an open invitation to the exploitative instincts of "civilized man." Except for the lofty mountains in the interior, the whole region was heavily forested. Towering evergreen trees, the result of mild temperatures and heavy rainfall, stretched in unbroken ranks from salt water beaches to the snows of the mountain peaks. These primeval forests so impressed the men of the U.S. Coast Survey that, in their 1858 report, they refered to "the immeasurable sea of gigantic timber coming down to the very shores." Spruce and cedar grew upon the river bottoms: the uplands were covered by stately stands of Douglas fir and hemlock. Many trees exceeded ten feet in diameter and rose skyward more than two hundred and fifty feet. On the moss-carpeted ground beneath them grew luxuriant ferns, vine maple and rhododendron. Wildlife was abundant, trout and salmon filled the swift, icy rivers; the tide-washed beaches teemed with oysters, clams and crabs.

This rich land was not unclaimed, however, because seafaring Indians resided along the shores in dwellings shadowed by the towering trees. These primitive people fished the coastal waters. They cruised the ocean in cedar dugouts in quest of seals or the Tyee salmon, and sometimes the hunters ventured far out to sea to harpoon whales.

In the winter the land was gloomy and forbidding. Gray storm clouds darkened the skies for weeks, and continuous rains left the forests soaked and dripping. Then the mountains enrobed themselves in cloud and fog, withdrawing from the sight of man. But the long summer days were often cloudless, and the mountain snows gleamed with distant, dreamlike purity. Unspoiled, the land had for centuries lain undisturbed by the white man's exploitation, its landscape a scene of serene natural beauty.

The European Seafarer

Today the Olympic Peninsula is still sparsely populated, but its wilderness core is circled by settlement and development. Yet it was one of the areas of the Pacific Northwest with which white men first came in contact, partly because it stood between Puget Sound and the sea and could not be completely ignored. The acquaintance was casual, however, and for years the peninsula was virtually inaccessible except from the surrounding seas. The dense forests, incessant rains and lack of readily navigable streams closed the region to all but an occasional hunter, trapper or prospector.

As early as 1543, Bartolomeo Ferrelo, under orders from the Viceroy of Mexico, sailed along the Pacific coast of North America. Thirty-six years later Sir Francis Drake followed essentially the same course in the *Golden Hind*. Historians believe that neither explorer went north of latitude 43, near Cape Blanco, Oregon, and the reputed discovery of the Strait of Juan de Fuca by a Greek sailor in 1592 is believed to be merely a legend. In fact, another two hundred years passed before any genuine exploration of the northwest coast was made.

The earliest recorded notice of the Olympic Mountains is that of Juan Perez, a Spaniard who was cruising along the coast in search of new lands for Spain. On August 10, 1774, Perez sighted the trident-like summit of Mount Olympus and called it El Cerro de la Santa Rosalia.

The following year two other Spanish explorers, Bruno Heceta and Juan de la Bodega y Quadra, landed parties near Point Grenville, about thirty miles north of Grays Harbor. On July 14, 1775, Captain Heceta anchored his schooner, the *Santiago*, then went ashore and took formal possession of the land in the name of the Spanish king. Records were sealed in a bottle and placed at the foot of a white cross. This was evidently the first actual contact western civilization had with the soil of the Olympic Peninsula. On the same day, Quadra's sister ship, the *Sonora*, lay at anchor to the lee of an island off the mouth of the Hoh River, a few miles to the north. Quadra was visited by Indians in canoes who held up pieces of metal, indicating they wished to barter. Because he needed fuel and water, Quadra sent several men ashore, but the Indians promptly killed them and destroyed their boat for the iron and copper it contained. Saddened by the incident, Quadra then left, calling the island Isla de Dolores.

Twelve years later Captain Charles William Barkley, commanding an East India Company ship, anchored near the same spot and sent a boat with five men ashore for fresh water. They met a similar fate. Barkley called the stream Destruction River, but later this designation was given to the island, and the river was called the Hoh, after the Indians.

In 1778 Captain James Cook, an English seafarer, sailed by the peninsula while searching for the Northwest Passage. Cook named the northwestern corner of the peninsula Cape Flattery, but he somehow missed the strait and continued northward to Nootka Sound on the west side of Vancouver Island. There he obtained a valuable cargo of furs from the Indians for practically nothing. Cook then sailed on to China with the furs, and the following year he was killed by Hawaiians during a fight over a boat.

Less than a decade later, in 1787, Captain Barkley again explored along the Pacific coast and this time found the strait and named it after the legendary Greek discoverer. The next summer John Meares, a British sea captain flying under the Portuguese flag to avoid paying license fees to the East India Company, entered the fur trade at Nootka. He reconnoitered the strait and was welcomed by an Indian chief fishing with a band of his people at a little island near Cape Flattery. Meares called it Tatoosh Island in honor of the chief. On the fourth of July, Meares sighted the high, snowy peak in the interior of the peninsula and called it Mount Olympus after the Greek mountain supposedly the home of the gods.

Another Spaniard, Manuel Quimper, sailed into the strait in 1790 and explored the San Juan Islands and the coast around present day Port

Townsend. The following year Captain Francisco de Eliza, on a discovery mission for Mexico, entered the harbor of what is now Port Angeles. On the bay, protected by a sandspit known today as Ediz Hook, he found an Indian village and named it Puerto de Nuestra Senora de los Angeles (Port of Our Lady of the Angels). The name was gradually contracted to Port Angeles.

In 1791 Francisco de Eliza established a base at Discovery Bay and Lieutenant Salvador Fidalgo, a subordinate of Bodega y Quadra, set up a short-lived colony at Neah Bay. Although soon abandoned, this post had the distinction of being the first settlement of the white man in what is now Washington State.

Two important events occured in 1792, the three hundredth anniversary of Columbus' discovery of the New World. Captain George Vancouver explored Puget Sound and, impressed by its beauty and recognizing the economic value of the sheltered waterway, claimed it for England; and Captain Robert Gray, representing the United States of America, discovered what is now known as Grays Harbor, and entered the mouth of the Columbia River after many others had failed.

With the advent of the Americans, the Spaniards withdrew to California, leaving the English to contend with the Americans for the "Oregon country." Gray's discovery of the Columbia closed the book on the discoveries by sea. After that the explorers came by land—a vanguard that later expanded into the migration of covered wagons, the settlers who trekked westward over the Oregon Trail.

Explorers By Land

Adventurers by-passed the coastal Pacific Northwest for almost half a century following the explorations by sea late in the eighteenth century. The Lewis and Clark expedition, a notable exception, ended its long continental journey at the mouth of the Columbia, but the Olympic Peninsula remained wild and untraveled, though not unclaimed.

The United States negotiated a treaty with Spain in 1819 and another with Russia in 1824 which removed these countries from imperial contention in the Oregon country, leaving the United States and England to quarrel over the area north of the Columbia and south of latitude 54 40' N. After much wrangling the boundary was fixed in 1846 at the 49th parallel. In 1841, before the controversy was settled, the United States commissioned the Wilkes expedition to survey Puget Sound. Twelve years later hunters from the Hudson's Bay Company at Victoria entered the northern Olympics, becoming the first white men to penetrate these mountains to any distance.

Washington Territory was established in 1853 and Isaac I. Stevens, its governor, negotiated three treaties with the Indians in 1855-56, in which the Indians ceded the Olympic Peninsula to the United States except for some portions set aside as reservations.

Other than Mount Olympus, none of the mountain peaks on the peninsula had been distinguished with a name. In 1856, however, a surveyor named George Davidson was impressed by the peaks visible from Puget

Sound. He named Mount Constance for Constance Fauntleroy, sister of his sweetheart, Ellinor, whose name he gave to a lesser summit near Lake Cushman. He also called a conspicuous, double-peaked mountain The Brothers, in honor of Edward and Arthur Fauntleroy.

For the most part, however, the Olympics remained unknown territory right up to the end of the nineteenth century, more than a hundred years after the first seafarers sailed along the shores. Although settlement had taken place along the Strait of Juan de Fuca and Puget Sound, no one except an occasional hunter, trapper or prospector ranged through the densely forested foothills surrounding the mountains. These men left no records or trails, and the mountainous interior was still mysterious and unexplored.

The First O'Neil Expedition

In 1882 Lieutenant Colonel Alexander Chambers, Twenty-First Infantry, United States Army, stationed at Fort Townsend, endeavored to penetrate the mountains behind the fort and construct a trail. After six months of difficult labor his party abandoned the project while still in the foothills. Three years later, however, Lieutenant Joseph P. O'Neil was attracted "by the grand noble front of the Jupiter Hills." O'Neil persuaded the commanding general, Nelson Miles, to organize a reconnaissance party. On July 16, 1885, a detail of eight men under command of O'Neil started from Port Angeles "because of its seeming nearness to the mountains" and entered the northern Olympics. The pack train consisted of four mules, later increased to eight. From Port Angeles the explorers, guided by an Indian, followed an old, ill-defined trail toward the foothills. The Indian deserted them when he realized where they were going, and neither promises of wealth nor threats of death induced him to remain. With reluctance he camped with the party at the base of the mountains, but slipped away quietly during the night.

Undeterred by the Indian legend of the Thunderbird who would inflict terrible punishment on transgressors of his sanctum, the party followed the course of Yennis Creek and hacked a path through dense forests, choking underbrush, and around windfalls, precipices and canyons. The men struggled slowly through the foothills and up the northern slopes to the high country overlooking the Strait of Juan de Fuca. Excursions were made from here in various directions, the main exploration being to the south and east along the crests of the higher ridges.

Wildlife was abundant in the mountains. From the beginning panthers prowled about the expedition's camps, frightening both men and mules, and great herds of elk, almost as tame as cattle, roamed the mountain meadows. The explorers also encountered an occasional black bear, one lone wolf, and numerous marmots.

Lieutenant O'Neil was impressed by the view from a high gap above Port Angeles. Snow-covered mountains, extending well above the timberline, rose in "wild, broken confusion" to the east, west and south. O'Neil picked out what he thought was Olympus, the highest point in a cluster of snowy peaks to the south, a mountain range that apparently circled on itself. "There is no regularity about their formation," he wrote of the Olympics in general, "but jumbled up in the utmost confusion, and the only regularity which does exist is that the ranges nearest the Strait and Sound seem to run parallel to those bodies of water, and with all their irregularity, ruggedness and at present difficult to access, the day will come when the State of Washington will glory in their wealth and beauty."

In the high country the party divided into two groups. One, under a man named Hawgood, left to explore toward the Elwha, but lost some provisions crossing a stream and had to return. The other, led by O'Neil, proceeded southeasterly to the divide separating streams flowing north to the strait and east to Hood Canal. The men then explored the headwaters of the "East Fork of the Elwha" (probably the Lillian, but possibly the Hayes) and got far enough south to see the source "and the field of ice from which it started." In this remote area one member of the party lost his way and was never found.

Although O'Neil's expedition did not cross the mountains, it aroused speculation as to what the interior contained and kindled interest in various plans for further expeditions which came to nought. But O'Neil's party made a beginning and was to be followed within five years by a more ambitious operation, the Press Exploring Expedition.

The Press Expedition

"Washington has her great unknown land like the interior of Africa." Thus did Elisha P. Ferry, governor of the newly created state, preface his remarks when he declared, in 1889, the "advisability of having the area between the Olympic mountains and the Pacific ocean explored." The mysterious interior of the Olympic Peninsula, untrodden by the foot of civilized man, afforded a fine opportunity for someone "to acquire fame by unveiling the mystery which wraps the land encircled by the snow capped Olympic range."

Because the mountains presented rampart-like walls on all seaward sides, men believed the streams draining them rose only on the outward slopes, none originating in the area enclosed by the mountains. Supposedly a great central basin contained a large lake that drained, via a subterranean outlet, to the sea. The unexplored region was also rumored to consist of "rolling prairies on a huge plateau." Game was abundant, as were minerals, and the whole paradise was guarded by fierce, hostile Indians.

Such tales aroused interest in exploratory missions and several groups planned to enter the Olympics in the summer of 1890. However, the party organized by the Seattle Press stole a march and to them went the glory of the first crossing of the mountains, during the winter and spring of 1889-90.

The party of six men and four dogs left Seattle in early December, 1889, for Port Angeles, "to ascend the mountains by way of the Elwha pass." They expected to live largely off game, but packed 1500 pounds of provisions with the help of two mules acquired at the last minute.

By Christmas the expedition was camped in a canyon along the Elwha River west of Port Angeles. After a great snowstorm the weather turned cold and the men kept a monster fire going day and night while they built a crude flatboat from frozen green lumber. When launched on New Year's eve, the boat promptly sank, but the explorers hauled the vessel out and recaulked it. This time it floated.

In freezing weather, the men towed the boat, laden with their supplies, up the icy Elwha. After twelve days, however, they reached the end of what they believed to be navigable water. Here the boat was abandoned. The explorers were forced to backpack their supplies, with the assistance of the mules. However, while the expedition was crossing the face of a mountain spur known as the Devil's Backbone, one of the mules fell over a cliff and was killed.

In late February, the expedition reached "The Forks," then the limit of exploration. The men pushed slowly ahead, plagued by the incessant rain and snow. When spring came the party was camped in a little mountain valley. Here the explorers lived mainly on fresh meat and fish, but as they moved deeper into the mountains, the country became rougher, the snow deeper and game scarcer. Their remaining mule, exhausted from the ordeal, finally gave up, unable to go further. The men and dogs, also near exhaustion, pushed on.

The explorers left the Elwha, which appeared to trend in the wrong direction, and labored up the canyon of the Goldie River. Their packs, stripped down to sixty pounds each, contained only essentials, and their clothes were rags, but hope was in their hearts that they would soon reach the Quinault and a path back to civilization. Their provisions were getting low, their starving dogs stole the last of their bacon, and the canyon became increasingly precipitous. Their progress slowed to a crawl, and in an effort to cross the mountains quickly they threw away a lot of useless equipment.

The expedition arrived in the heart of the mountains at the peak of the avalanche season. In constant fear of slides, the men climbed steep snow-covered slopes, and upon reaching a high vantage point were "almost stunned by the sea of mountains across the path" to their journey's end. Eventually they reached the top of a high divide, only to discover they were within the confines of a vast curve of the Elwha. Obviously a descent of several thousand feet to the river was necessary before an ascent could be made to the true watershed. James H. Christie, the expedition leader, reported this disagreeable discovery gave rise to "sundry hard expressions not usually found in Webster, but quite excusable under the circumstances."

From the Elwha valley, using ropes, the explorers climbed rock cliffs to the Low Divide. Their food supply, now reduced to nothing but flour, was nearly gone and time was running out on them. At the divide they found two small lakes, and near them a stream flowing south. Almost immediately the dogs flushed a dehibernating bear. The men shot the bear, then fried bear grease all day, and drank it as fast as it was ready, ravenous as they were for fat. While camped in the mountain pass they killed two more bears in the next few days, and thus saved themselves from starvation.

Anxious to get out of the wilderness, the men hurried down the Quinault valley, and fought their way through endless thickets of brush in dense rain forests. Ragged, battered, half-starved and nearly barefoot, they stopped long enough to build a raft that would, they hoped, float them down the river. The raft struck a log jam, however, and was swamped. Miraculously, all survived the incident, but most of their equipment was lost. Somehow they managed to save their diaries and films and the invaluable topographical map their historian, Captain Charles Barnes, had made of the mountains.

On May 19, 1890, a white man and two Indians canoeing up the Quinault picked them up and carried them downriver to the lake, then to the ocean where they hired a team to take them to Grays Harbor and civilization. It had been nearly six months since they had disappeared in the wilderness on the lower Elwha. Shortly afterward the men returned to Seattle and the Press published a detailed account of the expedition. The first crossing of the Olympic Mountains was history.

Later Expeditions

The Press party was followed in the summer of 1890 by a second expedition under Lieutenant O'Neil. This group, composed of soldiers from the Fourteenth Infantry and members of the Oregon Alpine Club, crossed the southern part of the Olympics from Lake Cushman to Lake Quinault, and explored the mountains on all sides. The lieutenant reported that one party led by B.J. Bretherton, the expedition naturalist, succeeded in climbing Mount Olympus and noted that its immensity made the surrounding mountains appear insignificant although they were only about a thousand feet lower.

In the next few years other groups explored segments of the Olympics. C.A. Gilman and his son ranged the length of the peninsula for the National Geographic Society, Judge James Wickersham and his family explored the eastern Olympics, and at the turn of the century a government party spent three years in the mountains surveying a new forest reserve. Thus within a decade the veil of mystery was lifted from the white peaks, although untrodden spots remain in the Olympics to this day.

The various exploratory parties named many geographic features of the Olympic Mountains and some of their nomenclature has survived the passage of time. Their chief contribution, however, was disproving the rumors. The Olympics did not contain a central valley or a plateau of rolling prairies covered with lush grasses. Nor was there a great lake with a subterranean outlet. The mountains were lacking in important mineral deposits, and no fierce Indians guarded the mythical paradise of rich lands awaiting settlement. Furthermore, the rivers were found to originate in the interior, not on the outer slopes of the mountains as had been supposed. The greatest surprise, however, was the discovery that the Olympic Mountains were not a range, but a jumbled cluster of precipitous, snow-burdened peaks.

PIONEERS OF THE OLYMPICS
by Lois Crisler

Following the Press and O'Neil expeditions, the pivot of pioneering swung from physical hardship on the frontier to daring on the social frontier. The last of the pioneers of nature followed the Press party accounts in the paper to the last frontier on the continent. Some of these pioneers are still living—barrel-chested Pa Huelsdonk, "the iron man of the Hoh," for instance, a man having a natural genius for pioneering, as another man might have for music. The odder, lonelier men who preceded them are gone—old bachelors in the forest. There was a man who toted his violin for company when he walked the trail from Indian Valley to Port Angeles for groceries once a month, sitting down against some fir trunk now and then to fill the lonely forest and the ears of surprised deer and cougar with reels and melodies that meant a whole world of people and ideas to him, and that vanished without effect among the vast branches. There was the old fellow who wanted to raise chickens and pigeons, and foreseeing their tender interest to skunks, hawks, and wildcats, made two holes in his cabin, one high, one low, for them to enter. The chickens roosted nightly on the foot of his bed and when they fell asleep, he turned them around to face the head of the bed. Lonely queer traceless little lives, but those of men who enjoyed the forest.

Back in Washington, D. C., pioneers of another kind were interested in the forests. For three hundred years, on an apparently inexhaustible continent, men had been killing everything that moved or lived its own life. Either it competed for their food or it was their food. That attitude was part of the old "pioneer spirit." The new pioneers were beginning to fight to hold onto the remnants of what had been hated and wasted. The continent had been choked with wilderness. Now the wilderness was getting scarce. And wilderness is very valuable. Its chief values are intangible but as specifically useful as those of "trace" minerals in food. Under Gifford Pinchot a national forest commission was set up during Cleveland's administration. And presently the new pioneers came to the Olympics.

Meanwhile the Press party's "rat hole" was looking like the robbers' cave of Sesame to lumbermen who had gutted the forests of the east. And when Henry Gannett, Chief Geographer, showed up in the Olympics from Washington, D.C., to organize a survey for a national forest here, the Senator from Washington State growled in Congress with anxious anger, "Why in God's name do these scientific gentlemen from Harvard have to come out here and butt in on our affairs?"

Henry Gannett one clear spring day found two lean daredevil surveyors, Dodwell and Rixon, and with two aides for them, climbed Mount Ellinor, on the east side of the Olympics. In the vast silence up there the five men looked westward over a sea of white peaks, azure distances, blue-hazed canyons cloaked with shining virgin forest. Gannett turned to the men: "There's your work, boys. Go to it."

They went to it, working sixteen to eighteen hours a day, packing their aneroid barometer and dry-plate camera to peaks, triangulating, running compass lines out, covering six to eight miles a day, noting the kinds of timber, and estimating its gigantic stands. In three years, they had made the original survey of twenty-four hundred of the ruggedest square miles in the country. And Jack McGlone, of their party, in 1899 had made the first recorded ascent of Mount Olympus.

It was as funny and characteristic in its way as the sourdough's pioneer climb of Mount McKinley over a decade later. McGlone, a little short Irishman, was working under Rixon, and when not surveying, just looking the country over, they lapped up twenty to thirty miles a day. Camped one September day at the head of Press Valley, now known as the Elwha Basin, they had climbed up through the Dodwell-Rixon Pass into the Queets Basin, then to the Quinault Divide, a very fair day's work for rugged men, and when they had circled back to the rocks above Humes Glacier, on the flank of Mount Olympus, Rixon called it a day, and prepared to start the two-hour hike back to camp.

Mount Olympus, rising radiant and massive at their side, had preyed all day on McGlone's mind. McGlone had an appetite for mountains, and under many a wild peak he had observed with delusive casualness, "I'll just be going up there to have a look around." Before Rixon could turn around now, McGlone had squirreled down the rocks and out onto the glacier.

"Come back and I'll go with you tomorrow," Rixon yelled.

"Too much trouble now, to get up those rocks again," McGlone yelled back.

The Irishman did not know what trouble was. There is one peculiarity about this eastern approach to Mount Olympus that makes it a major climb though a little under eight thousand feet. There is a steep, icy drop of seven hundred feet to the Hoh Glacier, before the real ascent can start. Rixon, watching the little dark figure moving up the Humes Glacier toward the evening sunlight, hunting a way around crevasses, saw him vanish from sight, just at the moment McGlone must have been discovering that peculiarity. Doggedly he went on.

The sun had gone down into the Pacific when the little Irishman took his "look around," alone on the virgin East Peak of Mount Olympus. The silent snow fields below him were satiny in the evening light; white peaks rose in every direction; and, dim on the blue eastern horizon, floated the pure volcanic cones of the Cascades. McGlone tucked a piece of newspaper, brought for a more useful purpose, into a tin can, built a little cairn over it, then headed for the Elwha Basin and blankets at two in the morning.

This first ascent was unknown to northwest mountaineers, and for eight years that scrap of newspaper rested undisturbed.

Getting sixty-five members of the newly formed Mountaineers Club of Seattle sixty miles into the wilderness, to Mount Olympus, in 1907, was first of all a job of trail building. Port Angeles came to the rescue. Diverse groups had rounded the long yellow spit that cleaves its deep still harbor from the blue strait, to float toward the wall of snow-topped mountains. Here, in

1865, had landed fifty war canoes with Neah Bay Indians in black bearskin robes, bearing red and blue blankets as gifts, for the wedding of a chieftain's son—men with their own ways of dealing with the dead and the living. Here, twenty years later, had landed a socialist colony, full of plans and traditions from Robert Owen and the Old World. There was an impetuous unanimity about the people of this town. When they jumped the military reservation, they jumped it "legally," that is, unanimously, in a Squatter's Association! When they ordered a drill, to tap what they hoped was coal, the whistle of the overdue steamer bearing the drill booped out as a politician was speaking in the opera house, and the whole crowd jumped for the door, leaving the embarrassed orator to wonder what in God's name he had said.

With the same unanimous financial zeal Port Angeles undertook to open a trail to the Elwha Basin for the Mountaineers. There was national publicity about this expedition for a proposed "first ascent" of Mount Olympus. Professors were going—to find new plants, new ore deposits. Who knew what might come of it? Impassively the Olympics waited. No one knew yet quite what to do with them; but there must be something. Port Angeles had the windfalls cut out of the old Press Party Trail up the Elwha and a new trail carried into the Elwha Basin.

The Mountaineers also had much to do. They bought pack horses, and for packers hired the Humes brothers, who had built a log cabin in Geyser Valley, the Press party's little paradise. By the first of June, pack trains were rolling up the Elwha, through the dim, level forest, with supplies to be cached in the basin: food that the wilderness bear would be too shy to molest; the 1907 version of mountaineering equipment—heavy blankets instead of sleeping bags, heavy canvas tents instead of hikers' tents. By July the personal dunnage of the climbers was going in.

Then, just a week before the Mountaineers were to start, one of those things happened to which there are always two sides; the ground was undercut from the Mountaineers' labors for the first ascent. Three men— Professor Herschel Parker, Belmore Browne, and a Mr. Clark—engaged one of the Humes brothers, a man innocent about "first ascents" but familiar with the new trail, to guide them to the basin. The year before, Parker and Browne had made an attempt on Mount McKinley. With Will Humes as guide, Parker, Browne, and Clark ascended the Middle Peak of Mount Olympus, swept out again and, with what seemed to the Mountaineers indecent celerity had an account in the papers of the "first ascent of Mount Olympus."

On August 12, 1907, L. A. Nelson, the leader of the Mountaineers, and two other men climbed the East or Sphinx Peak of Mount Olympus.—in "four hours and five minutes from Hospital Camp"—to discover in a little cairn a can with the lone Irishman's unsigned scrap of newspaper dated 1899. "We salute the brave pioneers who climbed in 1899," wrote the Mountaineers on their record, not knowing who had made this original climb.

The next day L. A. led nine men and one woman, Anna Hubert, to Middle Peak, where they examined the record of the Parker-Browne climb.

It ended with a doubtful admission that possibly a rock they saw to the west was higher. From the half mile of snow over the top of Olympus rise a number of rock peaks. Fog closed in as the party got down to the snow field; they scouted the confusing summit, the taste of cloud in their mouths. Three of them were up the black rock they took to be West Peak when the fog shifted to blue and there, a quarter of a mile away, rose the true summit of Mount Olympus. Within half an hour the Mountaineers were joyfully building a cairn on the hitherto unclimbed peak. They had won the game of first ascents after all.

A High-Rigger Hits Olympus

One more first was left on Mount Olympus—the first ascent of all three main peaks in one day. Officially, this record went, in 1933, to Dixon, a postman on vacation, passing his time by hiking. De facto, it probably belongs to the maddest man to climb a mountain, Tom Newton, a high rigger who became a legend even before his death. In 1920 he led three slick-shod, trembling youths over Olympus on a scouting trip for the Klahhanes, the Port Angeles mountaineering club. To Tom Newton everything on God's earth was expendable. It wasn't so much that he was reckless as that he knew his own prodigious strength. He could jump twenty feet down-ward and light on a rock like a cat, a leap it would break your jaw to follow. Lithe, with flawless balance and rhythm, when he topped a hundred-and-fifty-foot fir for a spar tree and the severed fifty feet dropped off, leaving the tree lashing in rebound, Tom would leap to the cut end and ride it, standing free, swaying against the sky. On Sunday afternoon, when other loggers played blackjack for pastime, Tom, for his recreation, would springboard fifty feet up a fir tree.

When he tackled Olympus, he had something worth his skill at last. He climbed it like a high-rigger. The men back-packed in from the Hoh River side and made high camp at Glacier Meadow alongside the Blue Glacier. In the morning Tom led up the Snow Dome. Under a cornice he hooked his fingers over and raised his body. "Sure! This is a good place," he called; and reaching over, gave each young fellow a heave up, to a steep snow slope with no trace of purchase; then an upward boost.

They climbed West Peak, and Tom stood on his head on the cairn. It made the men dizzy. He romped across the snow field to Middle Peak and on to East Peak, his party panting after. What was down he took at a leap; what was up, at a stride. From East Peak, without an instant's pause Tom plunged over the side, so steep you couldn't see below the bulge, down toward the Hoh Glacier. His shout drifted back, "Come on!" So he was still alive. One by one the men sat down and whizzed out of sight. The one left alone on the peak was Herb Crisler, a boy from Georgia, who had never been in the mountains before. "You can't stay here and freeze to death," he thought. "This is it," and over he went. Tom's shout roared through the glittering rush, "Hey you, stand up there and jump that crevasse!" He made the six or eight foot leap and landed trembling, vowing in his heart if he ever got off this mountain alive, like an Indian he was through with white peaks. The thunderbird could have them. It was not mountaineering of course, but only Tom Newton's style, a high-rigger's bold delight in risk that skill could balance toward life.

Tom took the men down Hoh Glacier on a run, jumping crevasses and shouting as he went. It was a nightmare to follow him. They siwashed it on the rocks, beside the glacier that night, by a little fire of gray sticks, continually trading places by the fire during the night to keep warm. The next day the men toiled around to Glacier Meadow and their cache, but Tom included a side trip. He bounded up to Blizzard Pass and down to the Queets Basin to tell the Klahhanes not to bother, that he had climbed the mountain and there was little left up there worth coming for.

Tom Newton (r) on Mt. Olympus

AHLSTROM'S PRAIRIE

You showed me small things then,
drawing a dime-sized lens from your pocket.
The days were long and you and I walked.
The grasses were in flower.
It was the summer we met.

Sometimes now, we stay
at little motels in little towns,
and walk before dark past vacant lots.
Bending over the weeds, you name them,
scraggly plants with meager blooms,
not calling them weeds.

So why was I surprised coming back from the ocean,
to see you down on your knees
in a bog on Ahlstrom's Prairie,
hunting with the camera lens
something you knew was there.

Following you over the grassy hummocks of the marsh,
I saw at last the low leaves of the sundew.
The plant, ordinary to the naked eye,
was breath-taking under the lens.

Each red hair
was tipped with a sticky globe of dew.
It glistened on these glandular tentacles
covering the upper side of leaves.

That they were fragrant to insects—
that they drew small flies which got stuck—
that the edges of the leaves curled inward
and finished the feast—
were all new to me.

I was fascinated by the power
of quarter-inch leaves to lure insects
and survive in nitrogen-poor soil,
by the power of the lens to reveal,

by the power of you to draw me tired and bored
from the trail, to see all this
in the burst of the sundew.

— *Frances Fagerlund*

WILDERNESS AREA

"To That Solitary Individual"

The road begins to narrow; it is sparsely traveled.
You regret the comfortable monotony of telephone poles.
Above you, in green herringbone, the glacial peaks
are symmetrical as teeth. You enter a jaw, the palate
of which is the lake. In sun or rain it looks frozen.
                              It exists to remind you of sky.

It is here you abandon your car and enter the woods.
Your party slides between trees, thin as apparitions.
You go single file now, on a trail salted
with needles and cones. Each carries his choice of provision.
Some port a tent, some a canteen of water, one pockets
                    a knife; and one, oddly, a book.

The trees are taller than other trees you have known;
their steep trunks are naked; they repel the birds;
and birds are not frequent even among low growth,
for the sun is reticent. It glints through chinks, diffuse
as sun from slatted windows in a narrow steeple:
                              this is shadow's diocese.

This is a silent opera; travellers save
their breaths for ascent. Moss sponges up the sound
of footsteps and falling cones. A creak or crack
might be an insect; or your imagination
blundering past green scaffolds and unfinished framework,
                              through transient rooms.

Then, broken branches hedge the trail; a tree-trunk
lies across the path like a felled brontosaurus.
You help each other over it and are confronted
with a landslide, a whole piece of forest floor gone,
and, twenty feet below, a froth of water.
                              You dig your heels in

centuries-old turf. The nature lovers note
rare ferns and ivies. Geologists stuff
strange rocks into their pockets. The man with the book
quotes a poem. And the path, as you knew it would,
breaks off suddenly, like a snapped branch:
       you face uncharted forest.

Here is where company parts: discards map,
compass, knives, poems. Each man yields
to lucky hunches, gleams, prehistory,
an animal intuiting his destination.
When the rain starts, drop by drop, it hits your face,
       a clarity. It freshens

cedar and moss until they are plangent as a word.
They are the words in this place: touch and taste,
see and smell. You are in the wilderness.
You calibrate its messages, all skin, like a plant.
Until awareness itself ebbs, and will sends down
      its roots; and root strikes heart.

— *Beth Bentley*

TRAIL TO THE ABANDONED INDIAN VILLAGE, THE OZETTE SITE

We leave the rain alone beside
the road where salmonberries loll
and a bird might be a snake

frightened by our breath. We call
each cloud a god, a white lake
of sleep where the dead redeem

us on this fern-dark path that will take
us to some shore. Drops gleam
on leaf ends and our hair.

Cedar once meant life here. Streams
taught trees to chant and charm the air
a million years of brown and green.

Alders whisper now, prayers
demanding why the wind was never mean
until those first tan sails

glided cleanly by, cut between
these people and their whales.
Skilled hunters, they knew them well,

spoke in heartbeats, sang before each kill
in apology, offered whorled shells
to wild men who lurked in wave and wood.

Our trail bursts open down a hill
of salal and clay to a beach that should
be Greece—bleached white

logs strewn like marble columns flood
our abandoned minds with flights
of Raven the Creator, his beak

carved in cedar, his blood bright
eyes gazing at the sea that speaks
and bends beyond our sense of time.

Its inhuman human hiss is our Greek
chorus, or a Salish curse on us. Sublime.
The trail tangles back toward gloom.

Somewhere our car cringes, mimes
the night. Somewhere the sea no longer hums
but chimes its Chinese bells, tide

reciting names of those who lived and died.

— *Edward Harkness*

THE OLYMPIC COAST: BETWEEN TWO WORLDS
by Tim McNulty

If each of the earth's wild places has its season—that time of year in which the beauty and power of a place seem magnified—then the season of the wilderness coast is winter.

Fall rains deepen the rivers for the fall and winter salmon and steelhead migrations, and offshore, at the river mouths, harbor seals can be seen feeding on the pooled salmon. Osprey and bald eagle will wait out storms in the wind-sculptured coastal spruces. One Christmas Eve, in the last light of dusk, I watched an eagle drop into the offshore swells and come up with a salmon almost as large as the bird itself. The salmon thrashed and fought wildly, eventually breaking free and falling, a silver fleck of light, back into the breakers. The eagle climbed to an almost unseen height, hovered for a moment, then dove once more into the waves. There was no way to be certain, but it surfaced with what looked to be the same salmon (not fighting as hard now), and flew low and heavily back into the dark trees.

Inland, winter clouds were settling about the broken, storm-battered crowns of some of the last coastal red cedar forests. Small creeks wound past the roots of trees that pre-date Columbus, and emptied over smooth-washed sands where gulls were bedding down for the night. Cedar was "Grandfather" to the original Northwest coastal cultures. Its wood split easily into planks used for their longhouse dwellings as well as for storage and cooking utensils. The great sea-going dugout canoes were of cedar, as were the decorative carvings. The pliable inner bark was used as fiber for clothing and baskets. Along with salmon, cedar remains one of the totem species of Northwest life.

The coast is ancient yet always new. It is a rich and varied interface between two worlds: the ocean world, its tidepools tiered with limpets and starfish, sea anemones and snails; and the shore world, where evening brings river otter, mink and raccoon to feed at those pools, and black bear and kingfisher stalk the water's edge. It was the subtly changing coastal environment that first brought life to our planet, and the limitless possibilities of that gift are played out daily in the waves and tide flats of the wilderness coast.

In late December and January, the storms come. Some may last for weeks, and it is then that the awesome forces which shape the edge of a continent have reign. Driftwood logs and trees loosed by the waves are tossed about like matchsticks, the racket of their clatter a strange undertone to the constant roar of the surf. Sitting atop a rock headland, one can feel distinctly the impact of the waves striking a hundred feet below, and might easily become soaked by the spray. It is this force, measured at greater than two tons per square foot in places, which finds the smallest weakness or fault in the bedrock and carves, over time, the magnificent seastacks and arches that so typify the Olympic coast.

Most of these stacks and arches, including many just now emerging, were formed long before the last Ice Age advance. As the ice receded, they were buried in glacial outwash and till. The sea coast then may have been as much as five or six miles west. As alder and willow began to recolonize these raw soils, and forests slowly migrated back to their northern sites, the seas rose and once more began their relentless quarrying. The vegetation and bits of forest that cap the highest seastacks and offshore islands are remnants of that age, witness to a ceaseless cycle of change.

Among the exposed bedrock at Point of Arches lies a section of rock dated at 144 million years, more than twice the age of the oldest known rocks of the interior. It is the only known exposure of its kind on the Peninsula. Some geologists believe it may have arrived here by way of a massive undersea rock avalanche from British Columbia while the Olympics were being formed. Others theorize it may have been rafted north from the Klamath Mountains of Northern California, a result of the ongoing processes associated with the San Andreas Fault. Its true origins, however, remain a mystery.

A half mile inland in the lee of a low ridge, an ancient cedar grove occupies the marshy ground by the outlet of a hidden lake. Storms have topped the cedars numerous times and some of them lift more than a dozen silver wind-scoured spires into the gales. A particularly ferocious windstorm in 1978 brought one of these old patriarchs to the ground and I spent hours exploring the bent and gnarled limbs and spires of its crown. The whole forest seemed permeated with the rich scent of the fractured heartwood. Looking about me at the size of this small sheltered stand and how few of the great trees lay prostrate, I guessed that possibly only once in a person's lifetime would one of these trees fall, and just as seldom would one of the many younger trees need to survive to maturity to maintain stability in such an old stand. Survival like this is rare along the Olympic's stormy coast and the vast majority of inland old-growth cedar stands have long since been logged off. These remaining cedars, protected by the Park, retain something of the soul of the ocean coast, something that belongs to all of us.

Winter storms: I remember the first and last time I misjudged their wrath. I was fording the Ozette River one December on a hike from Shi Shi Beach to Cape Alava. I'd carefully timed the tides so that I'd reach the mouth of the Ozette at dead low. A major storm had moved through the night before, but the surf remained ferocious. The Ozette, a gentle knee-high wade in summer months, was now holding its own against the whitecaps. I'll never forget the sound—or the feel—of the boulders and river rocks rolling over my boots, or the windy salt spray against my face as the force of the swollen river held the breakers at bay. I had to cross far down the beach where the widening of the river mouth reduced its depth, and the immense cresting waves seemed poised at my elbow. Needless to say, I felt about as close to winter sea as a two-legged ought to be—maybe closer— and it was only while breathlessly pulling on warm clothes, safe on the opposite headland that I noticed the raucous laughter of a flock of crows in a nearby spruce. For them it was apparently quite a spectacle, and they seemed to be enjoying it to the fullest. For myself, it would take a warm stove and a hot pot of tea somewhere miles ahead, before I'd be able to look back upon the occasion with anything but dread.

By February, the first long breaks in the weather bring the earliest of the spring shorebirds, and the thunderous rhythms of the winter's storms give way to a gentler music. The first bloom of Indian plum is soon followed by pioneer violet and the early blossoms of salmonberry. On a clear day in mid or late February, you might sight the first gray whales sounding and diving just offshore, following the same migratory route to the Arctic that they have for countless thousands of years. And if you are fortunate enough to find yourself on this all-too-rare and incomparable wilderness coast, perhaps you might feel something of what the first human visitors felt at the sight of the first northering whale. To the "coast people": Makah, Quileute, Quinault, it was not merely the return of another season, but the untold gift of life itself.

It is a gift which surrounds us still, in our cities and houses and cars, but nowhere so fresh, so beautifully whole and complete, and nowhere does it speak so clearly to those who will listen, as in wilderness.

CONTROVERSY

Olympic Gray Wolf—EXTINCT

A NATIONAL PARK IN THE OLYMPICS...1890

by James Wickersham

Judge James Wickersham's 1890 family expedition into the then little-known Olympic Mountains was the first to explore some of the high river-source region and to descend the Dosewallips River. Greatly impressed by what he saw, Judge Wickersham made the first known proposal for an Olympic National Park in letters dated November 3 and 8, 1890. He wrote: "A more beautiful national park cannot be found."

While exploring the upper Skokomish in July 1890, he met Lieutenant Joseph O'Neil's party which was engaged in making the first extensive reconnaissance of the Olympics. O'Neil also had a deep appreciation of the beauty, flora and fauna of the mountains and concluded his 'Report ...of His Exploration of the Olympic Mountains': "I would state that while the country on the outer slope of these mountains is valuable, the interior is worthless for all practicable purposes. It would, however, serve admirably for a national park." His report was dated November 16, 1890, and was published in 1896.

Until last summer [1890] these mountains had remained unexplored since the dreadful day of Seatco's wrath. The density of the forest growth at the base and the frightful canyon's walls at every point kept out all the white explorers, and so little was known that no map had located the streams falling out of these mountains. In July and August six of us—three gentlemen and three ladies—made a journey through the central plateau from which flows four large rivers. Our party examined all the rivers, high peaks, and hitherto unknown beauties of the Olympics. For 20 days we climbed mountains, waded torrents, slept above clouds, and, for the last seven days, lived on water and flour cakes, carried our provisions and luggage on our backs, and braved the wrath of Seatco, as well as all the usual fatigues of such a journey.

In all of the great commonwealths of Idaho, Montana, Nevada, Oregon, Washington and Alaska, there is not a national public park. The forests are being felled, and destroyed, the game slaughtered, the very mountains washed away, and the beauties of nature destroyed or fenced for private gain. The beauty of Switzerland's glaciers is celebrated, yet the Olympics contain dozens of them, easy of approach and exhibiting all the phenomena of glacial action. A national park should be established on the public domain at the head waters of the rivers, centering in these mountains. It should be 30 miles wide, north and south, and 40 miles east and west, containing 1,200 square miles or 768,000 acres, which is about one-third the size of Yellowstone Park. It would include the highest lands of the Olympics, the headwaters of all its rivers, the glaciers, Olympus, Constance, the snowfields, mountain meadows, grand canyons, and the homes of the last remaining elk, deer and bear. It should include Lakes Cushman, Quinault, and Crescent. The average height of land in the park would be about 4,000 feet, while many peaks would reach 8,000 feet.

The president of the United States has ample power under the twenty-fourth section of an Act of Congress, approved March 3, 1891, entitled, "An act to repeal timber culture laws, and for other purposes," to withdraw this region from disposal under the public land laws, and set it apart as a reservation. There are no surveyed lands within its boundaries and no private rights yet acquired. It would not withdraw any agricultural lands from settlement. Within its limits are large tracts of Alaska cedar, a very rare and valuable wood, as well as dense forests of cedar, spruce, hemlock, and pine. The census reports of 1880 contain full information concerning the dense forests on the foothills of the Olympics, which extend in many instances far into the interior, along valleys and lower levels. The heaviest forest growth in North America lies within the limits of this region, untouched by fire or ax, and far enough from tidewater that its reservation by the government could not possibly cripple private enterprise in the new state, and by all means it should be reserved for future use. The reservation of this area as a national park will thus serve the twofold purpose of a great pleasure ground for the Nation, and be a means of securing and protecting the finest forests in America.

FOR THE FIFTIETH ANNIVERSARY OF OLYMPIC NATIONAL PARK

You leave it to mark
where you were: a penny you hide
on the stairway of the Statue of Liberty,
a centime on the Eiffel Tower,
initials, hearts, a groove in sand till high tide.

Other places themselves mark a spot
so vast, you are the little thing
left behind. There, you stand at a wide window
watching the day turn dark,
facing the future.

Facing the future, the earth turns a shoulder
and we give that shoulder a name. It thrusts out
an arm: in the shadow we stake a claim.
For the world to go slowly, it takes
these spots in our vision, or whoever says.

— *Marvin Bell*

A REASONABLE PARK

President Roosevelt has come and gone, and he has an impression of the Olympic Peninsula, its communities and people he could have obtained in no other way than by a personal visit. He concludes that there should be a park in the Olympics, but he will give study to its boundaries, which is exactly what the people of Grays Harbor have desired.

On one hand, there are park extremists who would like to lock up the whole Peninsula, or a great and vital portion of it, depriving the people of the Peninsula of its resources and their means of livelihood. On the other, there are those who want no park at all and would subject the Peninsula to immediate commercial exploitation. There must be a point between these two extremes that will satisfy both the need of preserving the beauties of the Peninsula forever and at the same time afford a reasonable opportunity to those dependent upon the Peninsula to use the material that nature has provided. It is that point which should be reached in the controversy and if the president's visit assists in reaching it, the Peninsula will be grateful. There never was any need for the vast park that Congressman Wallgren proposed in his first bill and which he now may revive, and even his revised bill presents a park far too big because the beauties of the Peninsula can be preserved without it.

— *Aberdeen Daily World*, October, 1937

THE GREAT HOH ELK SHOOT OF 1937
by Murray Morgan

Around the turn of the century there appeared a group that advocated preserving much of the Olympic National Forest as a park, so that future generations could enjoy true wilderness.

Leaders of the total-preservation conservationists were particularly anxious to save the herds of Olympic elk, the largest and most stately members of the deer family. These were then being killed in large numbers by professional hunters, who sold their teeth as watchfobs to members of the Benevolent and Protective Order of Elks.

Representative Francis Cushman of Tacoma sponsored legislation in Congress to establish Elk National Park. It failed. The state legislature in 1905 barred elk-hunting, but a bootleg supply of teeth continued to flow off the Peninsula for some years. Representative William Humphrey of Seattle introduced bills in 1906 and 1908 to create a game refuge, but neither passed.

In March 1909 Humphrey called on Roosevelt at the White House and talked to him, nature-lover to nature-lover, about the elk. That evening, just two days before leaving office, the President wrote out an executive order proclaiming Mount Olympus National Monument. It was a bully monument—620,000 acres, half of it forested, all of it closed to hunters and to loggers and miners.

In 1933 the State Game Commission, giving as its reason the danger of overbrowsing, opened a four-day season on elk. One hundred and fifty were killed, mostly big bulls. A national authority estimated that the strength of the herd had been depleted 20 per cent. The season remained closed until 1936, when, having modified the law so as to permit a selective season, the legislature opened one range for a limited hunt. The uproar over that was limited too. But in 1937 the commission announced that the season would be opened for eight days in October and November in Clallam and Jefferson counties, outside the monument. You could shoot bulls, cows, and calves, though not more than one to a hunter. A license cost five dollars, and you didn't even have to have your eyes examined. Some Hoh ranchers took out from the hills for the duration.

The impulse to kill something big must be very strong. Sportsmen came from as far away as Florida for the hunt on the Hoh. Hundreds of big-game hunters drove up from California. Men who had never hunted before came to get in on the kill. I was working in Hoquiam at the time, and I remember being in a hardware store, talking to a city policeman, when a man came in and told the clerk he wanted to buy a gun.

"What kind of gun?" the clerk asked.

"Well, I'm going elk-hunting," he said, and he showed his elk tag. "How big a gun do I need?"

The clerk just looked at him for a moment, his mouth slightly open.

"Would a .22 be big enough?" the hunter asked.

"No," said the clerk, and brought out a 30-30. "You'll need this heavy at least."

"Wonderful," said the hunter. "Now show me how to put the bullets in."

The policeman showed him how to load and told him about the safety. The hunter was very grateful. We watched him drive away toward the mountains, and the policeman said, "I feel like an accessory before the fact."

That was the year the sporting-goods stores sold out on red hats—red shirts, too. I remember men went into the woods wearing hats trimmed with red tissue paper, and some wore raincoats with red stripes. One old-timer came through town in the gaudiest get-up I ever saw. He had a red shirt and red pants and red hat, and he had painted his shoes red and the stock of his gun red. He had a donkey in the back of his pick-up truck, and he painted stripes on the donkey.

The hunters came with tents and trailers and boards for building lean-tos. A party of ten men from Elma had a big truck with a striped canvas top, and the truck bed was filled with hay to sleep in. That first weekend there were more than three thousand hunters in a thirteen-mile stretch along the Hoh. Cars were parked bumper to bumper in long areas near the stream.

Minnie Peterson, a pack-train guide, was in the sub-alpine country above the Hoh on the morning the season opened. "It was like a battle," she said, "or a Western. You'd hear a shot, then a burst of shots, and then shot after shot after shot for minutes on end. There was drifting fog and it seemed like gunsmoke, though there wasn't that much shooting really."

The elk were badly confused when the hunt began. They were far from tame, but they had grown accustomed to seeing men. Most of them had never heard a rifle. The herds would stand stupidly for a moment after the firing began, looking around slowly, staring at whichever members fell; then they would break away and race, single file, for the hills, the tawny patches of their rumps flouncing ridiculously. If a cow elk was killed, the calf would often stand by, bleating, while the hunters butchered her—or until someone remembered it was open season on calves too.

Carl Fisher, a rancher in the valley, counted 160 shots fired at one small band of elk that was spotted crossing a stream. The hunters missed the elk, but one of them shot Mrs. Fisher's pet dog. The Fishers had put bells on their horses, but they hadn't thought to bell the dog. It might not have helped anyway. A guide from Port Angeles had belled his horses and put white blankets on them, but the middle horse in the train was shot.

Sometimes hunters quarreled over whose bullet had felled an elk. Game Protector Fred Rice was called to a willow-bottom area where a woman from Centralia and a man from Seattle were in dispute. The man said he had wounded a bull and started to follow it. The woman said she had been standing in the willow bottom when the elk staggered into sight and she shot it. Rice ruled that the kill belonged to the woman, since she had fired the shot that felled it.

The Seattle man was a good sport. He said his party would help her pack the kill out. It was a nice gesture, marred a bit when one of the men disappeared with a quarter of the elk, and the game protectors at the check-out had to arrest the woman hunter for not having a license. Later she explained that she wasn't really guilty of illegal hunting, because the elk had already been dead when she fired that shot into its head.

On the fourth day of the hunt it began to rain, a real Hoh Valley rain with weight behind it. The sort of rain where the sky leans on the back of your neck. The wind rose, and the great trees creaked and moaned, and the streamers of moss hung clotted like seaweed when the tide is out. Thousands of seagulls rode in on the storm and began to feast off the entrails of the elk.

The rain fell harder and harder, and the river began to rise. Many hunters started back for town. Under the sound of the rain and the trees they could hear the grinding mutter of the Hoh, rolling the boulders in its bed. The first to leave got out safely, though at some points the river was already over the road. Those who delayed were trapped.

Bucking the outgoing traffic was a truckful of hunters who were returning to pick up four elk they had killed in a swale across the Hoh from the Jackson ranger station. They were very eager, and when they reached the ripple where they had forded the river previously the driver stepped on the gas to get a good run. The truck just disappeared. Three men got out alive and made shore, but the driver drowned. He left a wife and six children. His body and the truck were recovered in the spring.

The Hoh continued to rise. Hunters who had cached elk beside the stream returned to find them swept away. Those who had crossed the river came back to find it impassable. They stood on the bank and watched the water come up over their parked cars on the far shore.

Some Indians with canoes were brought up by truck to retrieve the stranded hunters from the far bank. The rescue went well until one of the Indians noticed a raft of late-running salmon stranded in a pool that had formed in a campsite. Rescue work stopped until the fish were taken.

It rained for twenty-four hours; about ten inches of rain fell on the Huelsdonk ranch, where there were measuring devices. Then the sky cleared. The Hoh, which is very swift, drained quickly. The hunters who wanted to quit were able to go home. Others showed up to take their places. They brought word of a tragedy down at Forks. The state liquor store, the only one for miles, was out of whiskey. A hunter could still get gin, though.

When the season ended, 5280 hunters had killed 811 elk, which was about two hundred more than the game commissioner had anticipated. No one knew how many were wounded. Two professional hunters were hired to track down the cripples and dispatch them. The hunters had paid $26,400 in license fees, and they had spent an estimated quarter-million dollars on food, liquor, guns, equipment, and towing charges.

One night some weeks after the season I met an old settler whose ranch had been in the line of fire during the battle of the Hoh. We were in a tavern. I bought him a beer and expressed sympathy. He bought me a beer and assured me I was wrong. The elk season had been the most wonderful thing that had happened since Social Security. You see, he'd had a cow—old sick cow. Poor damn cow. And when the season opened he took that poor old critter out in the woods and tied her to a stake, and then he climbed a tree. Some danger, but not much. Pretty soon—bang! But she didn't suffer at all. The hunter was a good shot. Right smack between the eyes. Fellow from Seattle, he was, and pretty rich. He was most terribly sorry about killing a cow that had won all those ribbons at the Grays Harbor county fair. He paid $135 right there, and he wrote out a check for $200. Didn't bounce either.

The old settler dipped his beak into another beer. After that feller from Seattle was gone, he allowed, the old woman and him, they propped that poor damn cow up and got her leaning against a tree, and that week she earned $1425.37, three rifles, a spare tire off a pick-up truck, and she had twelve elk tags on her.

After the season he melted her down for the lead.

AN OPEN LETTER TO HAROLD L. ICKES, SECRETARY OF THE INTERIOR

Dear Mr. Ickes,

An unfortunate situation, which you could correct to the immediate benefit of all concerned, has arisen in connection with the proposed ocean extension of the Olympic National Park.

In the path of this extension are a small number of pioneer settlers who fear they are about to be evicted from their homes on your orders to acquire their lands by condemnation if necessary. Granting that federal title to these lands may be necessary in order to complete the park extension, it surely is not necessary to disturb the settlers' current occupancy. Lifetime leases, such as exist in other parks for similar situations, could be given.

It seems inconceivable that continued occupancy of these few ranches, mostly entirely removed from the main highway, could be seriously objectionable to the present generation of park visitors.

It is hard for those of us who have lived much in cities, moving frequently, to appreciate offhand the intense attachment developed by isolated settlers for lands which they have cleared and improved with their own hands. The unusual difficulties of carving a home out of this frontier wilderness naturally have accentuated that feeling. These people who do not want to leave their homes are just as naturally distressed as refugees abroad.

While some owners still may not want to sell, definite knowledge that they can have the purchase price and still remain in their homes, whether ranches or resorts, should dispel the principal difficulty. So far they have received no such assurance.

A word from you at this time would relieve the naturally distressed feeling of these settlers caused by the present uncertainty. It would also stop the current widespread publicity about "aroused settlers protesting eviction from their homes" which is causing unnecessary harm to the national park.

Additional harm is being done by agitation that the Queets corridor will be an impassable barrier against hauling logs to Grays Harbor from timber north of the Queets river. An official statement from you, confirming verbal assurances of park service men, that rights-of-way will be guaranteed across the corridor in both directions should do much to counteract this unnecessary alarm.

Respectfully yours,

Charles N. Webster, publisher,
Port Angeles Evening News
Port Angeles, Washington
March 26, 1940

THE PROPOSED OLYMPIC NATIONAL PARK
The Last Chance for a Magnificent and Unique National Park
by Willard Van Name

Willard Van Name had committed his whole life to saving trees. During the 1920's he was the lone voice who railed against the Park Service's continuing efforts to trade forest lands in the national parks for "scenery" which an eager Forest Service was only too happy to provide in exchange.

Van Name discovered that the Olympic Loop Highway had just been completed and that this road was going to enable the Forest Service to begin their long delayed clear cut cutting of the Olympic forests. Instead of focusing directly on elk, he focused his report on saving of trees and thereby saving of the elk habitat. When nothing at all happened as a result of his report, it seemed to Van Name and Edge that the climate in the Roosevelt New Deal might be right for an Olympic Park campaign.

He mailed a copy of his report to each member of Congress, every politician in Washington State and anyone and everyone he could find an address for.

— Carsten Lein

The completion, several years ago, of a motor highway entirely around the Olympic Peninsula, Washington, often called "our last frontier," which contains one of the largest unsettled areas left in the United States excluding Alaska, and the present employment of federal emergency funds for constructing new roads that traverse formerly wild parts of the Peninsula, has brought about a crisis in the history of the region, and makes it imperative to act promptly if we are to save any considerable part of its magnificent forests from annihilation and its wild life from extinction.

For preserving the game animals of that part of the country this Peninsula affords an ideal place. In its central and western parts the Roosevelt elk, the largest and finest variety of the elk, still survives in some numbers, and this region affords the only practicable place (in United States territory at least) where there is any hope of permanently preserving this magnificent animal. There do not seem to be any reasons why, with adequate protection from their human enemies, the moose, mountain sheep and mountain goat might not be permanently established there. Black-tailed deer and bears are still found in considerable numbers in spite of relentless hunting.

These are, however, by no means the only, and not really the most important and urgent reasons for protecting the area. The Peninsula affords the last opportunity for preserving any adequate large remnants of the wonderful primeval forests of Douglas fir, hemlock, cedar, and spruce which were not so many years ago one of the grandest and the most unique features of our two northwestern-most States, but which everywhere have been or are being logged off to the very last stick. Soon hardly an acre of such forests will remain anywhere to show what they were like.

Forming the extreme northwestern corner of the United States, the Olympic Peninsula is a roughly rectangular area averaging about 60 by 90 miles in extent, which is bounded on the west and north by the Pacific

Ocean and the Strait of Juan de Fuca, on the east by Puget Sound and the Hood Canal, and on the south in part by Grays Harbor, so that it is surrounded by ocean or tidal waters on every side except on the southeast. It is partly due to this isolation and partly to the character of the region and its climatic conditions that its settlement and commercial development have been retarded and so much of its wildness preserved.

We already have in the north central part of the Peninsula a reservation that will make an excellent nucleus for the National Park that we need. This is the Mount Olympus National Monument, having an extent of over 500 square miles and including Mt. Olympus and the surrounding high mountains. It was originally established as a reservation of the Department of Agriculture, but has lately been transferred to the care of the National Park Service.

This National Monument, established by a proclamation of President Theodore Roosevelt of March 2, 1909, was formerly of about double the present size, extending farther west and very much farther south, and containing a large amount of splendid primeval forest.

It was to get possession of this forest, and to be able to sell the timber that the Forest Service secured a proclamation (dated April 17, 1915) from President Wilson, cutting the Monument down to its present size and eliminating all the finely timbered parts—a striking example of the way the interests of the nation are sacrificed by bureau officials. Of course President Wilson had no knowledge of the Olympic region and did not understand what he was doing, but was relying upon the advice and recommendations of the Forest Service.

Another important respect in which the present National Monument is a failure is that it does not protect Crescent and Quinault Lakes. Fine lakes are very scarce in the western United States, and these two with the forested mountains and ridges around or near them should be strictly preserved from any more damage, as they are of very unusual beauty.

The Mount Olympus National Monument lies in and is surrounded on all sides by the Olympic National Forest, which is in the charge of the U.S. Forest Service. As in the case of all the other National Forests the timber of the Olympic National Forest will eventually be sold and cut for lumber. In fact that process has already been going on at certain points, but owing to the inaccessibility of the region has not yet proceeded very far.

The National Forest never did contain much of the best timber of the Peninsula, this having mostly already passed into private ownership before the time of its establishment, and having been mostly logged off, some of it many years ago, some more recently. Much of the National Forest is far more important to the nation for park purposes than for the small price the timber will bring, and should be incorporated with the existing Monument into a National Park before logging ruins it and defeats that purpose.

It is self-evident that the Olympic Peninsula stands in great and immediate need of more conservation for its wild life and natural beauty. It is also evident that action now can save far more and at less cost than if we procrastinate, even for only two or three years. More roads are penetrating into the central wilderness, bringing settlements, hunters, logging, the establishment of recreation resorts, and other destructive developments where all is wild and beautiful now.

We must keep in mind the fact that the purpose of the proposed park is to protect things that would otherwise be destroyed, and that the mistake of limiting the park (as was done in the case of Mt. Rainier Park) almost entirely to high barren mountains, should not be made.

For the Olympic Park we want representative areas, and good big ones, of the big timber, the wonderful Douglas fir, hemlock, cedar, and Sitka spruce forests of the northwest, no adequate samples of which are now being preserved anywhere.

Assuming that under present conditions any extensive purchase of land for the park will be impossible and that it must be created from the National Forest, and assuming also that the National Monument will be its basis, we need to extend the boundaries of the latter to the west and south well down the valleys of such streams as the Sol Duc, Bogachiel, Hoh, Queets, and Quinault to take in tracts of good forest (which does not grow in the higher altitudes) and to take in the shores of Lake Quinault (except the southwest shore). An extension to the north to take in Lake Crescent and some important parts of the Sol Duc watershed seems also necessary.

Those in favor of the National Park point out that the Olympic National Forest does not belong either to the Forest Service or to the local residents of that part of the State of Washington. It belongs to the American people as a whole. The preservation of such a magnificent animal as the Roosevelt elk is a matter of interest to the whole nation, in fact to the whole world. It is vastly more important than the privilege of a few residents to hunt on the lands which the American nation, not the residents of the Peninsula, owns. The same reasoning applies to preserving in its natural scenic beauty a reasonable amount of the primeval forests, and to protecting against diversion to private use of the especially beautiful spots that the public owns and should be free to enjoy.

There is not at present any bill in Congress for an Olympic National Park.

But if the Mt. Olympus National Monument were to be restored to its original extent we would again have a large part of the region we need for the park. As one of the chief purposes of the establishment of the Monument was to provide an effective elk refuge, and as the trimming to which President Wilson's proclamation subjected it has defeated that purpose, it is possible that his proclamation was illegal, and that only an act of Congress could thus trim down the area of the Monument. There was no such act of Congress.

However this may be, unquestionably President F. D. Roosevelt has the legal power to restore the Monument to its original boundaries by proclamation, and the public ought to be compensated for areas in the original limits that have been ruined by logging, by adding other National Forest lands that are still unspoiled and finely forested.

Letters to the President and resolutions by organizations asking that he make the above proclamation may be of important help. Action is needed at once, for plans are announced for the immediate extension of a logging railroad up the Hoh valley into some of the finest remaining timber.

LOGGERS' LOOT IN THE OLYMPICS

by Lois Crisler

The people of the United States own some virgin forest in the Olympic National Park in the northwest tip of Washington State which the lumbermen are determined to get. The nature of this property and some of the methods being used to obtain it are something its present owners ought to think about.

The Olympic National Park is a clump of wilderness mountains with low-lying rain forest on their west side. On the coastal strip between mountains and Pacific Ocean falls the heaviest annual rain in the U. S.— about 150 inches. The climate is mild. Snow is not common. The whole coastal strip, including the rain-forest acreage in the Park, provides some of the great tree-growing land in the world.

Since few people nowadays have seen virgin forest, it is worth describing. Ancient or virgin forest has rooms. One enters a forest room or, larger, a hall. One definitely leaves it, by a division of leaves and brush. Often in a "room" the great trees causing the shadowy overhang are hardly noticed. It is rather the forest light, the delicate white things—deep-forest flowers— and the mossy logs, or the hanging gardens of fern, moss, and flowers on the maple trees, that attract one's eye.

On the main trails there are "halls." Across the rivers away from the trails there are even lovelier old-forest effects. One passes from brush-scrambling into coppery glades. The copper color comes from the moss which covers the floor of the glade and usually the vine-maple trees as well. Sometimes one finds a still, spacious gold-green "hall" with a roof, a floor of moss and distant furniture of logs. There may be glimpses of graceful elk.

The rain forest has three levels. The roof, of Douglas fir, spruce, cedar, is 200 to 300 feet overhead. The mezzanine floor of big-leaf maples is 75 to 100 feet high. Near eye-level are wickets and arches of vine maple. Moss coats the floor, fallen logs and maples—often so thick that you can plunge your hand to the wrist in it. Up the maple trunks, cylindered thick with moss, and along the velvety limbs 50 feet overhead, ride growing ferns and flowers.

A striking feature of the rain forest, and one mentioned by President Roosevelt when the Park was established as unique and worthy of preservation, is the young trees growing along fallen logs. In this moist mild climate the fertilizing disintegration of the old trees prospers the growth of new giants.

Warning from the Lumbermen

In the spring of 1947 the Aberdeen, Washington, newspaper, which usually expresses the viewpoint of the lumbermen, stated with naive bluntness the program and intent of the lumber companies. It said that people will just have to learn to get along without seeing virgin forests anymore.

The publicity men have tactfully sugar-coated this "education" for the public. They do not say to the American people, "No, no! Baby can't have old forests. Papa wants that." They say, "Look! See the pretty new forest!" It is always well to note the technique of thought-control, especially when it is being used to try to take away one's own property. The main techniques of the lumbermen's publicists are five: (1) A special "loaded" vocabulary. (2) Invoking the mystic benediction of Science on all the lumbermen do. (3) Pictures showing how pretty young forest is. (4) The theme, "It's good business." (5) Ridicule of conservationists, while cautiously claiming for the lumbermen any virtue the word may still have. Let me comment on these points in order.

1. The vocabulary is that of farming, applied to forests. "Timber is a crop." It will get "overripe" and "rot" if it is not "harvested." It must be "weeded."

Thus the concept "forest" is replaced by the concept "timber." Now timber on privately owned land may be a "crop" if the owner desires. In a national park it is not a crop; it is a forest entity that can be wiped out in a few years and can not be replaced in a thousand. A climax forest is a biome, a biotic whole—fragile, living, a community. Its oneness has impact on the human spirit. The natural feelings of a person in a great virgin forest are awe and delight. These are valuable experiences. The lumbermen are taking some pains (by double-page color ads in national magazines) to smash down these feelings as improper and misinformed.

Forests Are Not 'Crops'

A farmer's crop is harvested when it is mature or ripe. A tree "crop" is "harvested" when the interested group considers it economically advantageous to do so. A Douglas fir may be 600 years old, as sound as a dollar and still growing. But in their wildest dreams lumbermen never consider letting a fir stand more than 120 years; 50 years is the time usually allowed.

The "overripe" trees in the virgin rain forest ultimately fall and are absorbed into the forest economy. In this wet, temperate climate young trees seed themselves along the top of the prostrate giant in the open patch of sunlight and grow, nourished by their ancestors. Moss covers the log; it sinks into the ground, fertilizing it for future generations.

Removing the "ripe" trees seems reasonable to people who do not know the fabulous rain forest. Young trees are crushed by the fall of a big tree and tilted aside and torn up by the giant as it is hauled out by caterpillar. The only kind of selective logging practical in virgin rain forest is clearcutting certain tracts. This logging is unbelievably ugly, and wasteful beyond conceiving to people who know only open forests in drier country. A single cut from a big tree—a short log that would make a full load for a sixteen-wheel logging truck and trailer—may be discarded because of one burl near one end. It would take a person an hour to clamber in a beeline up and down across a hundred yards of discard—"uneconomic" logs and waste—around a donkey-engine on a logging show. This in addition to the destroyed younger trees on the path along which the big tree was dragged out.

Science as a Cloak

2. Using the cloak of science is a good technique for public relations. Lumber companies need good public relations. They have had a bad record up to now. In 1907 there were 469 million acres of virgin forest in the U.S. In 1923 there were 138 million acres. The annual burn was 20 to 30 million acres, most of it the result of fires caused by logging operations. Now (1955) there are 44,600,000 acres. The annual overcut above the annual regrowth of trees was 400 per cent. In 1947 the annual overcut in the Olympic National Forest adjacent to Olympic National Park was stated by its supervisor to be 350 per cent.

The lumber companies are mending their ways, slightly, because no trees grow on the Pacific Ocean. They now use 25 per cent more of the forest waste than they did ten years ago—not an extravagant improvement, but a good sign. They make a big display of each improvement, naturally without indicating the size of the improvement in relation to the size of the nonimprovement. "Tree farms" are especially good medicine for public relations. (It used to be "reseeding"!) "Tree farms" are good lumber practice but minuscule as yet in comparison to the amount of cut-over land. In other words, there is improvement in logging practices but it is about one twenty-fifth as big as the public is led to suppose.

3. It keeps the publicity men jumping to show pretty pictures of clear-cutting because clear-cutting in the rain forest is hideous. And the pretty pictures of second-growth, or young, forest are usually taken from above. A person on foot inside a young forest is not bowled over by awe.

4. As for business, breaking the park would give the last giant "peeler" logs to the lumbermen. They would last the mills only about ten years or less. After they were used up the mills would perforce modernize their equipment to use smaller logs. Meanwhile the people would not even have to "learn" to get along without seeing an old virgin forest. There would be no problem, since such a forest would not exist now nor in the lifetime of forty generations to come, if ever.

True, after that the same number of board-feet might still be grown to the acre. But that is where statistics and reality differ vastly. The wood would be in numerous small trees, not in half a dozen forest-sheltered giants. However, logging practices good or bad should have no bearing on the forest the people have set aside for themselves and their children.

Who's Old-Fashioned?

5. As to ridicule, conservationists are presented as neo-druids dripping tears, myopic and old-fashioned. Lumbermen are "modern." They are "dynamic" conservationists who cut trees "scientifically." It is worth noting that among the "old-fashioned" conservationists who object to giving the Olympic National Park forest to the loggers are the Washington State Federation of Labor, consisting of 780 organizations; the International Woodworkers of America, C.I.O.; the General Federation of Women's Clubs, with 6 million members.

For scientific studies the biome, the whole that a virgin forest is, has values. It also has a value which is scientific but not measured, indeed hardly realized till today: the effect of wilderness on human psychology. Civilization up to now has been shaped by and predicated on a margin of wilderness. If authentic wilderness (that is, in large areas) disappears, we shall have destroyed the nurse of our most strength-giving characteristics—humbleness, awe, impersonal love for and delight in life independent from ours, running a course different from ours.

The values of wilderness were always there, even while men could afford to note only its feeding and danger aspects. But the time for "conquering" wilderness is past. It is so scarce now that it is time to protect it.

— *The Christian Century*
27 August, 1955

FOR THE VISITOR ON
THE LAKE ANGELES TRAIL

You say I don't love it enough,
that, living in the heart of hills,
I've become indifferent.

I think of fern digging in its root
deeper for the careless blessing of shade
from cedars tall in their greed for light,

how the brook works its sound over stone
before retreating underground
to rise again, secret, in stems of plants.

What you say I don't appreciate
is like my own breath, hard to catch
on this ascent to Lake Angeles.

Still, it rises with me each morning,
rests comfortably with me at night.

— *Nancy L. Beres*

OLYMPIC NATIONAL PARK CONTROVERSY
by Robert W. Kaune, Jr.

As the 19th century approached its close many people of this country were becoming concerned about the indiscriminate use of our natural resources.

The "cut and get out" logging practices of earlier years in the Atlantic States were beginning to be felt in the great "inexhaustible" forests of the West. Uncontrolled mining and grazing began to take their toll on the land. To those who thought of the future, a system of land and forest reserves was needed for a young and growing nation.

One of the greatest forward steps in conservation was the Act of 1891, which set aside 13,000,000 acres in forest reserves, better known to us now as the national forests.

The Olympic Forest Reserve came into being on February 22, 1897 which closed an area of 2,188,800 acres, and was under the administration of the Department of the Interior. Not only did the reserve enclose dense coniferous forests of Douglas fir, hemlock, spruce and red cedar, but also elk herds and incomparable scenery.

In 1900 and 1901, the Olympic Forest Reserve was reduced by 711,860 acres, under the premise that the land was more suitable for agriculture than timber production. The heavily forested land deleted from the reserve was quickly utilized by three timber companies and two individuals who had little time for farming.

In 1905, the Forest Reserve became the National Forests under the U.S. Department of Agriculture.

The nation was not only concerned about the economic uses of its natural resources, but also of the intangible items of the land that could be set aside for the inspirational and recreational pursuits as well.

Conservationists asked protection for the most significant natural and historical areas of the country that were immediately endangered by adverse land uses. From this plea for protection of our national heritage, came the beginnings of the National Park System.

As early as 1890, parts of the Olympics were noted as worthy of national park status. Lt. Joseph P. O'Neil, who undertook one of the first expeditions into the Olympics, commented that, "It would serve admirably for a national park. There are numerous elk—that noble animal so fast disappearing from this country—that should be protected."

It was the plight of the Roosevelt elk that brought the first formal plea for a national park in the Olympics. In 1904, Congressman Cushman introduced a bill to create an Elk National Park of some 393,000 acres.

The elk were being hunted extensively for their teeth, which were used as ornaments on watch chains. Although the bill failed to stir public interest, it did prompt the state legislature to pass a law prohibiting the hunting of elk until October 1, 1915. An exception to the law permitted miners to kill elk at any time and it is interesting to note that many more mining claims were filed for in the Olympic National Forest as a result of this exception.

Theodore Roosevelt was a tireless supporter of the national parks. He was influential in the establishment of several areas of the national park system.

On the morning of March 2, 1909, Congressman W. E. Humphrey discussed the status of the elk of the Olympics with President Roosevelt. Humphrey said the elk were of value enough alone to permit the establishment of a Mount Olympus National Monument. Roosevelt replied, "Just prepare your order, Mr. Humphrey, and I will sign it." Roosevelt did and later the same day the proclamation was signed creating Mount Olympus National Monument of 610,560 acres.

The news of the monument created little opposition at first. However, it was soon realized that the President's proclamation had closed the monument to mining. Humphrey was besieged by the mining interests to get the situation reversed.

President Wilson's reduction of the monument by about a half after World War I was followed by a few quiet years, but this uneventful trend would be reversed by successive years of fury on the Peninsula.

In 1926 Representative Johnson introduced a bill similar to Humphrey's that would change the status of the monument to a park. The economic interests again came forth on the Peninsula and the bill failed to pass despite its active support from the Sierra Club and the Isaak Walton League.

In 1933, by an executive order, President Franklin D. Roosevelt transfered all national monuments that were under the administration of the Forest Service to the National Park Service. This action had far-reaching effects for Mount Olympus National Monument. Not only was President Roosevelt sympathetic to parks in general, but he had a personal desire to have established an Olympic National Park.

Numerous conservation groups took on new enthusiasm with this Presidential support and united for the many Olympic battles to be fought in the years to follow.

One group in particular, the Emergency Conservation Committee, stirred up controversy between opponents and proponents alike. In 1934 this group released a pamphlet entitled "The Proposed Olympic National Park."

As proposed by others before, the group called for a change of status for the monument and added the need for protecting the dense lowland forests, especially on the west side. The monument had really only protected the elk on their summer range. To some people even this was in question.

From this time on, the controversy would center around the final size of the park, not its ultimate establishment. Almost anything below timberline was declared too much by the opponents, and almost everything down to sea level was wanted by the proponents.

The first of three bills to establish a national park on the Peninsula, H.R. 7086, was introduced by Representative Mon C. Wallgren of Washington on March 28, 1935.

The bill proposed a park of some 728,360 acres which included most of the original monument plus some of the rain forest environment on the west side. The opposition called for a "sane and reasonable" park and their support for this view was backed by some 95 organizations which included various Peninsula chambers of commerce, labor unions, development leagues and industrial groups.

The Forest Service was also opposed to the Wallgren bill. Among the 44 groups for the bill were the Sierra Club and the Mountaineers.

The proponent list also included numerous individuals from all parts of the country. Formal hearings on the bill were conducted by the Committee on Public Lands of the House of Representatives in April, 1936.

The opposition prompted Wallgren into introducing a second bill, H.R. 4724, on February 15, 1937, which called for a park of 142,000 acres less than the first bill proposed. The Emergency Conservation Committee called the new bill a "double cross." The second Wallgren bill was obviously a compromise of sorts to both sides, but neither side was sold on its merits.

Up to this time the nation was not totally aware of the Olympic conflict, that is, until President Roosevelt made his well known trip to the Peninsula in 1937.

The President arrived on the afternoon of September 29 and was greeted by 10,000 Peninsula residents. That evening he gathered with various representatives from both sides of Lake Crescent and drew them into a common desire to have a large park established. A decision on the Olympic struggle was not far off.

On March 25, 1938, Wallgren introduced a third bill, H.R. 10024, which called for a park of 860,000 acres, plus 50,000 acres along the Pacific Coast from Cape Flattery to the Queets River. The bill formally adopted Olympic for the name of the park, rather than Mount Olympus.

The Governor of Washington along with many others protested the size and suggested the proposed park be trimmed down to 452,000 acres. The President was anxious to have the bill passed during that session of Congress, and he also indicated possible compromises to avoid a legislative deadlock.

Roosevelt recommended a park of 682,000 acres providing that he could expand the area up to 898,292 acres after conferring with the Governor of Washington and the Secretaries of Interior and Agriculture.

The day for the park proponents arrived on June 29, 1938, when the President signed the bill creating a 638,280 acre Olympic National Park.

— Port Angeles Evening News
February 7, 1966

COMMENTS OF DR. MICHEL BATISSE
Deputy Assistant Director, Science Sector, UNESCO
World Heritage Site dedication,
Olympic National Park, June 29, 1982.

On behalf of the Director General of UNESCO, I would like to first extend his greetings and congratulations to the government and to the people of the United States and of this particular state on the occasion of inaugurating the plaque, commemorating the inscription of the Olympic National Park on the World Heritage list.

Man in fact does not exist without nature and without culture. In other words, I think there is a Chinese proverb which says that man has to walk on two legs. Well, one leg is nature and the other leg is culture.

The breakthrough in this Convention is the recognition that certain sites—be they cathedrals or the pyramids of Egypt—or be they national parks like the one in which we are now, are in a way older than the nation where they happen to be located. They belong in a way to the entire world. They are part of the human heritage; and as part of the human heritage, it is the human community which has a responsibility for their long-term protection.

After all, we all remember that the first world national park which was established was Yellowstone back in 1872. This is really a symbol of what this country has done for nature conservation.

I would like to say that when the Olympic National Park was accepted on the World Heritage list, one little recommendation was added to this inscription by the International Committee, that the United States authorities should consider extending the nomination and protection to the very beautiful and unique shores along the Pacific ocean which were not in the original submission. I am extremely pleased to note that this has now been implemented.

The Olympic National Park is not only a site on the World Heritage list, but it is also recognized under another UNESCO program, which is called Man and the Biosphere Program, as what we call a Biosphere Reserve.. an area which is protected and managed for its representation of an ecological system. What happens in the protected areas can be compared with what happens in the areas around which are subject to various activities. This concept of the Biosphere Reserve is used here in Olympic National Park and this also, I think, is extremely important.

At the present moment, and as a Convention, we have 112 sites, either natural or cultural, which are on the World Heritage list.

A danger is the effects, the long-term effects of certain human activities on the future of the planet. I am thinking here in particular of what will happen if the accumulation of carbon dioxide in the atmosphere changes the climate. It requires maintaining the forest areas of the world as much as we can, and again perhaps the World Heritage Convention and the protection of such areas as the Olympic National Park have real significance in this respect.

The loss of genetic resources is absolutely fantastic and it is estimated that about 25,000 species will disappear by the turn of this century—both plants and animals. One of its (the Convention's) major purposes is to protect our genetic heritage in plants and animals. Olympic National Park has some unique plant and animal species which must be protected, not only because we cannot reinvent them or recreate them, but because someday we might need them.

The inscription of Olympic National Park on the World Heritage list is a heavy responsibility for all the people of this country, not only because of your own interest and the interest of your children, but because it is an example of what all countries should be doing.

PIONEERS

IRON MAN OF THE HOH

A mile at sea, Cake Rock, against the blue,
Lifts its seafowl sanctuary. Harsh squawks
   Float from the monoliths. A few
High breakers begin their crests and churns,
As I watch the sun sinking toward the sea stacks,
      And the world turns.

Again I've walked this tideline near La Push
From the Quillayute River to Hole In The Wall.
   Offshore the rocks, like gods, stand fresh,
Unshaken by all the ocean's worst in storms,
Their only voice in cormorant and gull:
      And the world turns.

A dozen times I've walked it with Applebaum,
Painter and raconteur. One time he told
   Me, with his monolithic aplomb,
As we strode along on shells and fish skeletons,
The story of the Iron Man of the Hoh:
      And the world turns

On such accounts. It seems this Northwest Samson
Carried an iron cookstove twenty miles
   Up the Hoh on his back, having
Homesteaded among Douglas firs, moss and ferns
In 1890. And as God made little apples,
      And the world turns,

Two loggers, who saw him trotting the stove through the wood,
Asked, "Isn't that heavy?" He said, "No, but it's hard
    To keep my balance on a log
When the sack of flour shifts in the oven."
So he raised his family far from any road;
            And the world turns.

This man, John Huelsdonk, killed 300 cougars,
Once had his leg lacerated by a bear,
    Crawled home 2 miles through firs and cedars,
And then walked 40 miles in to Forks.
His daughter pulled two men out of the Hoh by their hair;
            And the world turns.

My wife and daughter, at the tidal edge,
Move by Cake Rock, which now, against the sun,
    Goes purple-brown with the light's change,
Their pockets full of agates and odd stones.
My campfire gives the wind a pungent stain.
            And the world turns.

Well, I've seen Babe Ruth hit two home runs
At Navin Field, Frost at 75,
    Auden juggling the concerns
Of his century, Thomas in two taverns,
And Roethke, one of the giants of the alive;
            And the world turns

Into legend. I remember Jean Garrigue
Embracing a Douglas fir in the Rain Forest.
    Applebaum has fished among
Those basalt giants on which the seagull mourns.
Is that you, John Huelsdonk, where the breakers start?
            And the world turns

Purple-blue in dusk. I think of how
My parents loved, imagined, and endured.
    I gather wood and watch gulls float
On gathering breakers and settle on the crags.
The sun enters the ocean, a ball of blood,
            And the world turns.

— *Nelson Bentley*

DORA HUELSDONK—IRON WOMAN OF THE HOH
by Ruby El Hult

John Huelsdonk himself became impatient of the stories told about him, but as the "Iron Man of the Hoh," he has become immortal—in spite of himself. But little has been told of his helpmate of half a century, Dora Huelsdonk, who could with equal justice be called the "Iron Woman of the Hoh."

Consider the wedding trip of Dora Wolf Huelsdonk. She was an orphan who had been raised in the Huelsdonk family in Germany but had become separated from them when they came to America. When she herself came across the ocean there followed a reunion in Iowa where the Huelsdonks had settled. John, seeing his childhood playmate grown to young and attractive womanhood, fell in love with her. Later he came back from adventuring in the west to marry her and take her to the homestead he had selected in the Hoh Valley.

It was late in October 1892 that the newly married couple landed from a tiny steamer in a little cove at the mouth of Pysht River. There John hired a wild-looking Makah Indian crew in a dugout canoe to paddle them around rocky Cape Flattery and down the boiling coast line to the mouth of the Quillayute River.

The western slope of the Olympic Mountains is famous as the region of greatest rainfall in the United States. Here, as the winds of the Pacific Ocean strike the mountain mass and begin to lift they drop from 130 to 150 inches of rain a year. Up the valleys of the Hoh, the Queets and the tributaries of the Quillayute, in the wetness and warmth, march the great "rain forests," centuries-old fir, cedar and spruce, festooned with lichens and heavy mosses—an all but impenetrable jungle.

The rivers in this area are precipitous and temperamental, rushing torrents when the snows in the high Olympics are melting.

It was into this dark green, stately but forbidding wilderness that the Huelsdonks made their way, up the Quillayute River by Indian canoe, branching off and continuing up the Calawah. This itself was untamed, almost unknown terrain, but was only the beginning. Abandoning the river, they hiked along old elk trails and through jungle where there were no trails at all, crossing overland into the Hoh Valley. Here again they took to Indian canoe, which John poled up the river long miles into the forest, until they reached his homestead claim.

From Pysht, Dora Huelsdonk had traveled sixty miles by Indian canoe and afoot. Now at the end of her journey she saw above the high river bank, a little shack in a small clearing. Behind it, dark and ominous forests seemed about to shoulder this puny effort of man off into the waters of the Hoh. Here Dora Huelsdonk set out to create a home. Here her four daughters were born without benefit of medical attention. Here she knew and endured all manner of deadening drudgery, hardship, terror.

The isolation was supportable when her husband John was home to give some sense of security. The terror came when he was away, working in logging camps, hunting, tending his trap line, traveling to the Quillayute for supplies. Then she seemed trapped in the dark forest as in a maze without beginning and without end—a maze in which she would become uneasily aware of the dependence of her children on her, the only adult in this shut-away world. The thought haunted her: If some accident should befall her, what would happen to her helpless children? That was the piercing thought of more than one pioneer mother left alone in an isolated cabin where help was far out of reach.

The Huelsdonks had far more than the usual isolation; they also had the treacherous Hoh to deal with. When the rains came its waters became white and angry and no one could pole up its course or cross it. The only trail followed the north bank and at such times there was no way to cross over to the south bank where the homestead lay. If John Huelsdonk was away when the river rose he could not return home until the Hoh went down again.

By this time others of the Huelsdonk family had come to the Hoh. John's brother Henry had taken up a homestead farther up the river, as had John's father; and his grandfather, old and bedridden, was living with John and Dora.

The river was rising one day as John and Henry Huelsdonk started off downstream by canoe on a trip to the Quillayute. As planned they were to stop at the homestead of a downriver neighbor on some errand. A day later the neighbor appeared on the opposite bank and shouted across to Dora, and in the ensuing conversation she learned that her husband and his brother had not appeared at the neighbor's homestead. To her this meant but one thing: their canoe had been upset in the capricious river and both had been drowned. Crazed with grief, she nonetheless tried to hold some hope and to go on with her responsibilities. At the time she had two children: Lena, two, and Dora, a tiny baby in a homemade cradle. Milk was necessary for the children, and milk was also the only thing that the old grandfather (so ill he might die any time) could consume; and anguished as she was, it was necessary to go milk the cow. Before leaving the cabin she tied little Lena to the handle of the big trunk, then fastened the cradle to grandfather's bed so he could rock the baby if she cried.

Calling the dog she went off into the forest in search of the cow. She found it without too much difficulty, milked it, and then as she started to carry the full milk bucket home, apparently struck out in the wrong direction and became hopelessly lost in the dark tangle of trees. Frantic despair overcame her. Believing her husband and his brother drowned, knowing the old man to be near death and unable to rise from his bed, she saw in her imagination her babies, cold, starved to death, their little bones reposing by the trunk and in the cradle. For if she failed to return, there was no hope for them. Neighbors would not know of their plight, or if they did could not reach them across the raging Hoh.

Then it was that she thought of the dog. Calling him to her she ordered him home in harsh tones. Crestfallen he turned and ran off, then stopped in bewilderment. She followed after and again ordered him home. On his heels she stumbled into the clearing, sat down and wept.

Days later, when the Hoh went down, John Huelsdonk and his brother returned home. The unruly river had swept them past the neighbor's homestead but their canoe had not been upset. They were safe, unharmed, and came carrying huge packs of supplies. Life settled back into its old routine of land clearing, fence building, water carrying (by shoulder yoke with pails), of churning, of hunting, of curing wild meat, and of all the other endless tasks necessary to sustain life there on the edge of the rain forest.

With only two trips to the "outside" Dora Huelsdonk spent the rest of her life on the Hoh. She died in 1947, six months after the passing of her remarkable husband. They lie in the family cemetery on the upper Hoh, together in the shadow of the mountains which together they faced and conquered.

WHEN THE SETTLERS CAME TO THE WEST END
by Lena Fletcher

When settlers moved in to the west side of Jefferson and Clallam counties, it was very rugged and undeveloped. There were hardly any trails even to Forks and Quillayute, which were on prairies. Only a few trails, presumably natural, but actually of Indian construction, were kept open by yearly fires in early spring in the dead bracken ferns of the year before. I heard my father tell how he and his older brothers went to the Hoh by going along Indian trails from Port Crescent to Bear Creek, the Sol Duc, and then on to Forks. Their route is now suggested as the Lake Crescent by-pass.

The Indians and elk always knew and used the easiest grades and best passes and if one disregarded their routes, troubles multiplied fast. The West Side had some of the most impenetrable underbrush anywhere in the world excepting only the tropical jungles. In fact, the visible world to the traveler was reduced to a few feet, or often mere inches.

My father had worked at least a few years on the U.S. land surveys upsound and at Sequim before he set out on his first trip to the Hoh, so he knew his way around in a wilderness. When he went to Iowa to marry my mother, he and his brother Cornelius had already built a log cabin on 'Neil's homestead, and to this he took his bride, Dora Wolf, who had years before in Europe been his parents' foster-child (an orphan and one of six children).

They hopefully brought along a cow and calf, having been advised that there were plenty of elk ferns and willow sprouts for their cattle to winter over on—very possible, if it hadn't been for the exceptional snow of the 1892-93 winter. Nobody measured the snow in the Hoh Valley, but around the Hood Canal it was recalled as being seven feet with all growth except large trees smothered under a blanket of snow. By digging along hillsides and banks, the folks did manage to find ferns and other vegetation— enough to get their cattle through the winter. People in forests were lucky for the heavy snow pulled down branches of vine maple, willow and other edibles to within reach of animals. ...

For the first fall, winter and spring all groceries and commodities, chiefly tools, had to be backpacked to the Hoh from Port Crescent or Forks. People are always talking of living off the land, assuming there were endless game and fish to take. Well, at the time of the first settlement, what we call game was practically nonexistent. ...

After the first year, settlers on the Hoh had gardens, of course, and cows for milk and cheese. One could always get pork at Forks so we did have some meat. Also there were rabbits, grouse, and in season, ducks and geese. There were trout, and sometimes steelhead.

In the early gardens one found cabbages, carrots, many potatoes, and other common vegetables. People also raised grain: rye, wheat, buck- wheat—and oats for the poultry. Beans and field peas were commonly dried for winter use. We ate well after the first year of pack-everything-in.

The soil was fertile; "bugs" not yet imported, and most bad weeds still unheard of in those distant new places. One of the tedious jobs I remember was picking over the newly threshed grain to remove trash and then grinding it in a "hand mill" for mush or bread. The flour one bought in Seattle or Grays Harbor almost invariably was "buggy" and sometimes almost inedible.

TO THE BAILEY RANGE WITH BILLY
by Dr. Keith Thompson

After my family came here in 1910, we started vacationing at least one week each year up at Olympic Hot Springs. In those days people didn't have automobiles like nowadays. We rode out there in one of the Stanley Steamers that ran between Port Angeles and the Sol Duc. To go to the Hot Springs we took a road (currently Herrick Road) about a mile up the Elwha River on the west side. From there it was ten miles by trail up to the Hot Springs.

In the summer of 1917, we were taking our usual vacation. Billy Everett, founder of the Hot Springs, was a descendant of John Everett who, with his partner, John Sutherland, discovered both Lake Crescent and Lake Sutherland. They were Hudson Bay trappers and headquartered at Freshwater Bay, where the Everett homestead is today. Incidentally, Billy was born out there. When he was fifteen, he and his two hound dogs were roaming around the Olympics and discovered Cream Lake, located on the Bailey Range between Mount Ferry and the Hoh River. He called it that because the glacial silt from Mount Ferry settled into the lake basin, creating a creamy color when seen from a distance. Billy used to carry an Eastman picturecard-size Kodak for his wildlife photography. He took bear and elk pictures.

This particular summer Billy was going on a trip and invited Harold Thompson and me to go with him. We asked about food and blankets, and he said he'd take care of everything. To my surprise we didn't take blankets or food, excepting bread and coffee.

The first day we went to Oyster Lake on Mount Appleton. We ran into our first large herd of elk and our first bear near Oyster Lake. That's right on the pass where you go over and down into the Sol Duc. We spent our first night over in lower Cat Creek Basin where Boston Charlie, Billy's uncle, had a log cabin. Later Herb Crisler named this area Hot Cake Camp.

That night we learned how to "rough it." Billy built a fire near a rock or log, to reflect the heat back, and whoever got cold would get up and replenish the fire. We were reminded of Dewey Sisson's story of lying beside a log and shivering up a sweat. Actually, the body can do this to protect the inner parts. In shivering you generate heat.

The next day we dropped into Cat Creek, then followed up the branch that drains the glacier up on Mount Carrie. That second morning, when we took off, Billy pointed to a spot near the end of the ridge between Cat Peak and Mount Carrie, called the Cat Walk. He told us he'd meet us there that evening—and disappeared.

There's a little lake there where Boston Charlie had a mine on the Hoh side of Mount Carrie. A lot of quartz veins were showing in that area. You can still see the old tunnel entrances he dug there, looking for gold. But he never found any.

Mount Carrie was named by Theodore Rixon in 1900, while on a survey of the future Olympic Forest. He and his partner, Dodwell, were commissioned by Gifford Pinchot, one of the first Yale forestry graduates and first head of the U.S. Forest Service.

While traveling in this country, we were always on the lookout for treed blue grouse. Billy showed us how to throw rocks at the bottom grouse. The others would stand there and watch while you picked them off, one-by-one, starting at the bottom. That was to be our bill-of-fare, together with bread and huckleberries, for the entire trip.

Billy seemed to have pots hidden in various spots, so we didn't have to carry cooking utensils. He'd make a pot of coffee, and we'd all use the same pot for a cup.

We were amazed at the large numbers of wild pigeons feasting on blueberries on the mountain sides. When alarmed, a whole flock would take to the air and blot out the sun.

Our second night was spent in what is now called Seven Bull Basin on the side of the Bailey Range. Crisler named it that right after World War I, when he started building camps in the Olympics. Later he used these while making his elk pictures for Disney Studios.

The third day we left our camp and, staying above Cream Lake, camped at a smaller, un-named lake, now called Lake Everett. This lies below Mount Ferry, which was named by the Press Expedition for Governor Ferry, governor of Washington in 1890. There's also a peak near Boulder Lake called Mount Everett. These places were named after Billy's demise.

After exploring Mount Ferry Basin and looking at the glacier, which today is about one-third the size it was in 1917, we ran into the largest herd of elk I've ever seen. We sat on a rock promontory and watched them feed all around us, but the light was too poor for Billy to get any pictures. They were completely unaware of our presence.

On the fourth day we began the return trip, spending two days going out, whereas we took three going in. I'd learned how to "rough it," but in later years I enjoyed the luxury of either blankets or sleeping bag—and store-boughten foods, which today are actually taken care of by the dehydrated foods you can buy. This eliminates the need to carry flour, baking powder and lard for biscuits. It's all put up in one package as Bisquick.

THE MOWICH MAN TAKES HIS LAST TRIP TO CREAM LAKE, THAT HE DISCOVERED YEARS AGO

by Jack Henson

When Billy Everett, the old "Mowich Man" returned to the Olympic Hot Springs, September 26, from a ten day trip into the Cream Lake district of the Olympic mountains, he said that would be his last one so far into the mountains.

Seventy-nine-year-old Billy discovered Cream Lake when he was 16 years old, roaming alone in the mountains with a gun, salt and flour. As a young man he took "Boston Charlie," a celebrated Indian character of this region, in to see the wonderful game-haunted vast animal paradise, sprinkled with lakes and shadowed by the Bailey Range.

For the past four years Herb Crisler and Billy have been making the long trip into Cream Lake together and this year and some of the other years, Mrs. Lois Crisler has gone with them. Billy will be 80 years old in February and says he is not leaving the mountains entirely but has made his farewell trip into the far Cream Lake area.

As though sensing that the "Mowich Man" was not coming back to see them, two elk put on a great show of their fighting ability one day. A farewell gesture to an old pal. And then one night a lone bull elk kept the party awake, bugling near camp. Who knows but it was good-bye in the language of the wilderness. As daylight came, Billy watched the old lone bull pacing within 40 feet of the tarp lean-to and studying it suspiciously. He had an unusually fine bugle, "Like tapping the keys of an organ" as Billy put it. Most people hear only the distant whistle, but at close range like this, the entire song was audible, a rising falling sequence like do-mi-sol-la-heigh la-lal-fa-do, fingers on a flute. "The champion bugler of the Olympics," declared the old Mowich Man.

It is possible the elk herd nominated their champion to greet and say farewell to the old champion of them all, the old Mowich Man, who first penetrated their hidden paradise.

Now that Billy is in his late 70's, Herb has been helping him in with the grub weight, packing him into his old beloved haunts. The Mowich Man has carried his own pack of sleeping bag, pack board and personal equipment on the ten-day trips. On the first day this year, September 17, in addition to the other load he carried his own grub supply for the entire trip.

The story is told of Billy that once, when he was young and more agile, he was camped a mile through the pass from the lake and seeing a storm coming, made the trip all the way to the Olympic Hot Springs in a day with no trail, even down Boulder Creek. He took the down parts of the trip on a trot.

Although he has decided not to make the long trip into Cream Lake anymore, Billy will continue to go on his annual deer hunt into the Calawah area each fall to keep what he calls the "go-up-and go-down" in him. To keep in condition for the trip Billy clears an acre of ground each year and saws the wood for his Freshwater ranch.

At Cream Lake, Billy said, there is nowhere the number of deer or elk that were there years ago and no whistling marmot now. In his opinion there are more bear in the area than there were when he first went there.

On his last trip to Cream Lake, Billy's daughter, Jean, and her husband, Harry Schoeffel, made the one-day trip from the Olympic Hot Springs to the Cat Creek basin and all camped there overnight and returned together the next day to the Olympic Hot Springs that was also discovered by Billy and is operated by Jean and her husband.

Although I have taken a score or more trips with Billy in the hills, we have never been to Cream Lake together. It has been an education to view the high country with him. His eyes are still keen. Getting up before daylight and before the coffee has boiled or the bacon fried, Bill stands on the shores of Boulder Lake and in the dim morning light before the sun has sent its fingers over the encircling hills points out deer and elk that I cannot even see without the aid of field glasses. He follows their progress around the rim and up and over into the timber with vivid description of the animals and their habits.

Around the camp he hunts for dry wood to start the camp fire and rustles the heavier wood to keep it going. At night, scorning the shelter, he lies in his sleeping bag on the grass under the stars.

Every bird, bud and flower, as we hike along the trails and through the meadows, is fully noted and described and marveled at by the veteran.

At the end of the day on the streams, with a creel full of trout, Billy will set down, eat heartily, relax and tell stories of his youth and his trap lines around Lake Crescent and his home at Freshwater. He tells of the experiences of his father, John Everett and his father's trapping partner, John Sutherland. These two Hudson's Bay Company trappers from Victoria were the first white men to see the lakes that are now Sutherland and Crescent. Crescent was first called Lake Everett and the elder Everett had a trap line around it and Billy helped tend the trap line.

Although I have known Billy almost forever, as far as I am concerned, much of the material for this little story about Cream Lake was furnished by Herb and Lois Crisler. The fact of it is that I would like to give them credit for it all.

— *Port Angeles Evening News*
October 7, 1947

THE PREACHER'S SLEEPLESS NIGHT
by Svante Lofgren

One of the first settlers at the north end of Lake Ozette was August Palmquist, a young Swedish bachelor, who arrived in the spring of 1890. Homesteaders, who were mostly Scandinavians, kept coming during the early eighteen-nineties. Within a few years, quite a settlement had grown up on the north end of the beautiful eight-mile-long lake.

The need for a post office had long been felt when August Palmquist and a few of the other settlers made up their minds to see what could be done about it. The result was that the United States Postal Department appointed Palmquist as postmaster. However, the Postal Department furnished no one to carry the mail to the settlement's little post office, so the honorable postmaster himself had to pack the outgoing mail from Ozette to Clallam, and from there bring back mail for Ozette. As each trip made took not less than two days of hiking, and he had to make two trips a month, the postmaster served as pack horse at least four days every month.

But the postmaster did not complain. He was young, strong, and happy. He had not made many trips over the trail before he eagerly looked forward to the next time he could cover the same distance. The settlers wondered what made their postmaster so happy and so satisfied with his small pay and far from pleasant job.

News soon spread that he had fallen in love with Ole Boe's daughter, Annie, and had a chance to see her on every trip he made to and from Clallam.

Ole Boe was a Norwegian, who with his family had settled six miles from Lake Ozette at a place called Big River. Boe's place was right on the trail leading from Ozette to Clallam. Annie, the oldest daughter, was a typical blonde Scandinavian, fair as a rose, strong as a young bear, and always full of fun.

Annie promised to marry the young settler and first postmaster of Ozette. But there was no one authorized to marry, and they did not know what to do about it. Finally, one day when Annie tried to solve this problem, her thoughts happened to drift to the postmaster and storekeeper in Mora. Every settler had the highest regard for him and used to go to him for help and advice. Maybe he could help them.

The following day Annie knew August would be on his way back from Clallam with the mail, so she walked several miles to meet him, and they sat down on a windfall to talk it over. August considered it a very good idea and decided to go down to Mora the following day to see Olof.

The Congregational Church in Seattle had a missionary preacher, who occasionally came to Forks, La Push, and Quillayute to hold services. This preacher happened to be in the vicinity at the time, so Olof found him and stated the circumstances. The preacher agreed to marry the young couple.

Now the next question was how to get to Ole Boe's place at Big River from Quillayute Prairie, where the preacher stayed with some friends. From the Prairie it was eight miles in a straight line to Lake Ozette, no road, and a very poor trail blazed over the rough terrain by Olof a couple of years before. Since there was the possibility that the preacher would miss the trail and get lost in the wilderness, Olof promised to accompany him.

About four o'clock the morning of the wedding day, the preacher and Olof hiked over the trail to the south end of Lake Ozette, where they found a skiff Palmquist had promised to have waiting for them.

After about three hours of rowing, they reached the settlement at the north end of the lake. From there they had another hike over the six mile long trail to Ole Boe's place, where the bride and groom awaited them.

It was shortly after noon when they reached the Boes' homestead at Deep River. Olof wanted to start back as soon as the ceremony was over, but the newlyweds would not allow it. They insisted on having the guests stay and share the wedding cake and other good things they had to eat. It took at least two hours before Olof and the preacher started on the return trip.

The lake was still resting calm and serene. The young preacher's thoughts were absorbed in the beautiful scenery that surrounded him. He did not notice a black storm cloud which drifted in from the ocean and within a few minutes lashed the lake in its fury.

The preacher was struck with fear, expected the little rolling, pitching boat to sink, so he begged Olof to row to the nearest shore.

"We were halfway across the lake and to the end of my trail. We have nearly three miles to nearest shore, so nothing is gained by going to a place where we have no business. There is no trail around the lake," was the answer.

The preacher had no other remark to make, sat quietly, held onto the boat, and stared at the stormy water. His face turned white. Suddenly he started to vomit and feed the fishes his slice of the wedding cake ...and more too.

Olof felt sorry for the poor seasick man, but there was nothing he could do to relieve his suffering.

The storm ended just as suddenly as it started. Before they reached shore, the dark clouds had disappeared and the lake was bathing in the rosy rays of the setting sun.

Olof, who had done all the rowing, not trusting a land-lubber with the oars, thought they could reach the Quillayute country before dark if they started out on the trail immediately and walked as fast as they were able to go.

With this in mind they started out and got along fairly well so long as it was daylight and Olof could see traces of his overgrown trail. But it gets dark earlier under the giant evergreen trees, where the twilight shadows rest even in the middle of the day. When the trail disappeared in the darkness, Olof told the preacher to prepare to camp.

"Mr. Erickson, what have I to prepare to camp with?"

"Well, Reverend, watch me," answered Erickson, as he walked over to a large spruce tree, which was completely covered with long, thick moss, which he gathered and placed against a large spruce with branches nearly reaching the ground.

The preacher followed the example; but he could not understand how that could make a camp, until Olof spread out the moss and made a bed of it.

"Here is where I am going to get a good night's sleep," he said as he covered himself with the soft moss. A few minutes later he was serenely resting.

The preacher also lay down in his primitive bed. He felt comfortable, warm, but he could not sleep. Instead he was listening to the soft murmur in the high trees and the dying thunder of the surf breaking on the rocky shores of the Pacific.

It reminded him of an organ in a church far away. It sounded beautiful but strange, and he thought it would soon lull him to sleep. Just then another note was added to this orchestra of nature. The added note was confusing and discordant. He listened intently, but he could not make out the direction or cause of the noise.

The ghastly sound increased; it came closer; and he earnestly wished he had never gone with Erickson.

When he could stand it no longer he got up, grabbed Olof by the arm, and told him to listen.

"It is just the scream of a cougar calling its mate," said Olof, who simply rolled over and went to sleep again.

"Just a cougar!" the preacher repeated to himself. Just a cougar! Didn't he learn at school that the cougar or mountain lion was the most dangerous animal in the whole American continent from British Columbia to Patagonia? And that man Erickson completely ignored the danger.

The preacher wished he had a gun so he could protect himself in case the cougar attacked him. No cougar or other wild animal was going to find him lying down, so he arose and stared to walk around the tree.

The cougar's gruesome screaming and wailing gradually became less loud, and silence took its place after a while. That gave the preacher a chance to sit down to rest his tired legs.

He had been resting only a short while when another unfamiliar sound reached his strained ears.

Somewhere branches were cracking and breaking. It could be a deer or an elk, but it might also be a cougar or a bear. He arose to his feet again, renewed his walk around the tree, stopped and listened now and then, and tried to make his eyes penetrate the darkness of the night. Ever so often he could plainly hear something that was moving near him, but nothing could be seen before daylight started to break. Then he discovered a large bear in the underbrush.

The bear came closer, looked at the preacher, and stood up on his hind legs.

The preacher got frightened, grabbed Olof's arm again, and hollered, "Look! Look! See who is looking at you!"

Olof rubbed his eyes to get them open. He took a look at the big animal, who seemed to him larger than any other bear he had ever seen. He knew that most bears would not attack a person if they were left alone to tend to their own business. The preacher had rushed away the moment he let go his hold on Olof's arm, and he stood hiding behind the tree and cried, "My God, my God!"

After a few minutes, the bear tired of looking at Olof, put his front paws down on the ground, and lumbered off into the underbrush.

With the break of day and more light to see the trail, they continued their hiking. They had not gone far, however, before the preacher complained of weariness.

"Why didn't you sleep when you had a chance?" Olof wanted to know.

"Mr. Erickson, do you think I can sleep when there is danger all around me?"

"Danger? I don't know of any danger; you didn't get hurt did you?"

"No."

"I am not much of a Bible reader, but doesn't it say somewhere in the Good Book that even if I wandered in a dark valley, I am afraid of no danger because God is near me, or something like that?"

"Yes, but a person can't expect protection from above when he throws himself into the path of danger."

"Well, we have not done that, and we are safe."

The preacher changed the subject, and wanted to know if Olof were sure that it was a cougar they had heard during the night and not a person lost in the woods. And, if it were a cougar, why did he not attack them. Many people have been killed by cougars.

"That may be true," answered Olof; "but in most of those cases it was the person's own fault, or the cougar was so hungry that hunger forced him to tackle his greatest enemy—man. A cougar would much rather kill a deer or elk."

The good man, who never had studied the habits of wild animals, did not know what to believe or think. How did anybody know that a cougar preferred deer or elk meat?

However, the two men had not gone so very far before Olof, who was leading, stopped and pointed at a half-eaten young elk.

"The corpse was not here yesterday. Whom do you think killed it?"

"The cougar."

"Yes, the woods are so full of both elk and deer that there is no need of killing human beings."

The two wanderers reached Quillayute Prairie just in time for breakfast. The preacher told his friends about the adventure and said he would never again go out in the woods with Olof.

RIALTO AT DUSK

Something invisible lives here.
Mist writhes around driftwood
like Medusa's hair. A voice
crying (is it only a gull?)
causes you to strain for words,
as wind whines through the fir trees.
The steady boom of waves against rock
is the heartbeat of this place.

In an old photograph turned brown,
a lodge stands right over there.
Women, dressed in ruffles & such,
fine ladies from another order, lounge
on the porch, mustached men pose, hands
on hips. They called this beach, Mora,
but some things never change, despite names.

Now, as campfires dot the beach, darkness
drifts in, stealthy as fog, you
can almost hear the lost laughter,
see lights dancing on the ballroom floor.
Strains of music, frail as seafoam,
touch the air & vanish into salt rain.

— *Bonnie Nelson*

FIRST ANNUAL OUTING OF THE KLAHHANE CLUB
by Ben Phillips and E. B. Webster

At the end of the 19th century great numbers of Americans turned to the wilds for recreation. Rustic lodges and cabins were their retreats. For others hiking and mountaineering clubs provided avenues to nature. The Oregon Alpine Club (the Mazamas) and the (Seattle) Mountaineers made trips to the Olympic Mountains, and in 1915 the Klahhane Club was formed for outdoors lovers from the Port Angeles area.

Portions of the first annual outing of this club are presented here. Comparatively few people went into the mountains in those days; access was limited and camping was primitive and demanding. Outings were necessarily hard on the land—bough beds, campfires in alpine zones and attendant pack stock left their scars. Today there are many more of us using the wilderness and outing styles have necessarily changed. This account points up and contrasts those changes, underscoring the continuing need for us to "tread lightly upon the land," and yet, it provokes thought about what we have lost in our high-tech approach to outings today.

The outing outlined was from Port Angeles to Mount Angeles via Heart O' the Hills. The Burn was the recently burnt flanks of Mount Angeles; one hundred foot firs and hemlocks clothe the burn today.

Fifteen Klahhanes completed the outing. They left their lodge, climbed the Burn, spent several days finding a route through the Angeles Peaks, and spent a couple more traversing Hurricane Ridge to the mouth of Wolf Creek on the Elwha—a week of fun with a Forest Service promise of more trails to be built in 1916. Years later, the Klahhane Club is still making annual outings.

— Russell Dalton

These last years since Mr. Fisher cleared out the trail up to the foot of the rocks of the first peak, some two or three hundred people have visited the mountain each year. The club has engaged Mr. Fisher to cut a new trail around the east side of the peak, from the Burn, or sink hole, to the [Heather] Park, giving a long easy grade and practically eliminating the peak.

It is planned to leave Port Angeles on the afternoon of Saturday, July the 3rd, autos being furnished for the first three miles. The distance is seven miles to Klahhane Lodge, a half mile up the side of the mountain. It takes from two or three hours to walk out there being a good wagon road the entire distance. Shelter will be furnished in the lodge, and in tents, in case of rain, but each one if he has not already done so, will have to cut boughs for his own bed; it will be well to allow time enough before dark for this.

Sunday will be observed, as customary on annual mountaineer outings, as a day of rest and quiet for all of those who desire, with song service in the evening.

Monday morning, early in order to avoid the heat of the sun, each one will roll up his blanket, pack his personal effects, and hit the trail. Two hours is sufficient for the climb to the Burn, but there will be those who will take frequent and long rests, reaching the top after four or five hours. The outing committee will see that the slower members are looked after and that all reach camp in the Park. Here each one may make a bed of the thick alpine fir boughs in the immediate proximity of the camp, which will be located among the clumps of fir in the shelter of the ridge.

A big campfire will be held on the summit of the peak that evening, and on the following morning, assuming that the sky be clear, a side trip will be taken to the snow field of the Third Peak, returning to camp that evening. It is more than likely that the latter days of the week will afford an opportunity to acquire a little real mountaineering experience.

The outing is for members of the Klahhane Club only. But we expect to have as members of the club every person in Port Angeles who is interested in our great out-of-doors and in the development of our scenic resources. It will cost you an initial fee of one dollar to join this outing—and the club— and that dollar will be spent on the trail, which we are having built to make the trip easier for you. Should you wish to continue a member of the club, and we believe you will, the dues will be 25 cents per month.

It would be impossible to plan an easier trip reaching the same elevation to any point in the Olympics. Yet it is a camping trip and only those of average health who can get along with blankets, sleeping under the stars, and who are willing to assist with the work as well as participate in the pleasures of camping, should consider going.

It is intended that the Annual Outing shall be a feature of the Klahhane Club, visiting, each year, a different portion of the Olympics. A clear record for attendance at all annual outings held is a matter of considerable pride among the members of other mountaineering organizations; everyone intending to join the Club should make an effort to participate in this first outing.

The cost of the trip will not exceed one dollar per day and will probably be about seventy-five cents. Very little will be necessary in the way of special personal equipment for the first annual outing. It is hardly likely that we will have rain so near the strait in July; also, when on the mountain, we will be above the heavy rain clouds. There may be fogs; there will be heavy dews. For protection a piece of table oilcloth may be taken, or a heavy bed sheet can be used to advantage as a shelter. No matter how warm the day, it is always chilly on the mountaintop after midnight. One warm blanket, a suit of woolen underwear, and a flannel shirt or sweater to protect the shoulders, will leave little to be desired. The woolen underwear is worth more than an extra blanket. Two or more should combine in selecting their sleeping equipment, thus reducing the weight. Blanket or safety pins are desirable. There should be a good sized piece of mosquito bar for each bed.

The alpine fir grows short and very dense, its long, heavily foliaged limbs lying on the ground. Usually they grow in clumps of a dozen or more, so that a few minutes work with a hand axe will clear out a space, affording shelter from the wind, privacy, and a quantity of the finest boughs for a bed. Camps will be selected with special reference to these features.

As to clothing, any old wool suit or dress will prove satisfactory. Women should wear short skirts with bloomers or knickerbockers. The latter should be suitable to be worn without the skirt when climbing about the rocks. Men's peg-topped overalls make, with slight alteration, a dandy pair of bloomers; leggings should be worn unless one has high boots. Good, solid shoes are the one thing one must have. Be sure the heels are low; next to new shoes which have not been broken in by two or three days' wear, high heels cause the most trouble; they are positively dangerous. After breaking in the shoes a few large cone-headed hob nails should be put in the heels and soles; have the soles made thick enough so large nails may be used without possibility of punching through enough to hurt the feet. There should be a pair of light shoes to wear around the camp; tennis shoes will do. Both heavy and light hose should be taken. A small can of zinc oxide adhesive tape will prevent blisters. Bandanna handkerchiefs are handy, also a small flour sack to hold toilet articles, needle and thread and twine. An alpenstock may be made of a rake handle by inserting a sharpened steel point. Men should carry a hand axe, and women as well as men, a pocket knife. Each one must provide his own tin plate, cup, knife, fork and spoon. A pack sack will be necessary; those who haven't one may bring a burlap bag which will be made into one to fit their needs. Tents will be provided in case of rain.

Everyone joining this outing should take a camera for there will be almost unlimited opportunity for good pictures. Buy all the film you can afford, and then some.

BENJ. N. PHILLIPS,   ED. B. WEBSTER,
President   Outing Committee

AN OLYMPIAN TASK
by Bryn Beorse

Spic and span Douglas fir logs, fresh from a helicopter ride, nestle in the walls of the graying half-century old Enchanted Valley Chalet. It was originally built of ax-hewn white fir cut from the mountainsides.

Windows built by retired master carpenter Oiva Knute—the same man who built the originals—reflect the waterfalls and cliffs of the valley deep within the Olympic National Park.

Tired hikers open new, solid wood doors and shutters to visit the public emergency shelter in the chalet, where rustic furniture built a half-century ago still serves. Lots of tired people have sat on them after a 13.2 mile hike from the end of the road on the East Fork of the Quinault River.

The Olympians Hiking Club, a Grays Harbor outdoor organization, has completed its $20,000 project to restore the charming old three-story building that has served generations of hikers, rangers and outdoor-lovers.

Two years ago the chalet restoration was the largest cooperative project between the Park Service and a private group in the Pacific Northwest region. The job won a regional award for historic preservation and caught the imagination of hikers and non-hikers alike on the Harbor.

The chalet is a bit of an oddity in one of today's premier wilderness parks—a large building on land that by law is to remain forever wild.

Enchanted Valley chalet

The chalet was built by members of the pioneer Olson family from Quinault as a tourist lodge in 1930 and 1931. However, the Depression threw a shadow over the tourist trade. The building was next used as a lookout for enemy planes during World War II. It eventually became the property of the park. John Olson of Quinault says he hopes it will be placed on the list of historic places.

The club raised money by collecting aluminum, soliciting donations, conducting a pancake feed and other methods, while $1800 was raised by raffling off a donated Elton Bennett painting.

Just to bring in materials, food and equipment cost the Olympians some $7000 in helicopter time. Logs, donated by ITT Rayonier and sawn to fit by Mayr Brothers Logging Company of Hoquiam, came in one at a time beneath the chopper.

The only power tool used on site in the restoration work was a chainsaw.

Sections of the building were jacked up and braced. Two new doors were built, many new windows and a complete set of shutters were installed, a new chimney went up, security bars were bolted over windows for the ranger station section, some new flooring went in, a new roof hatch was built and wood preservative applied.

Today's concept of wilderness is new, and the Enchanted Valley Chalet is old. Dr. Alan Comp, director of the office of historic and cultural resources for the Park Service in Seattle, says that the chalet has a special place in the Olympic wilderness—one of the most extensive in the 48 contiguous states.

The chalet was built in expectation of a cross-Olympics highway, he said—a road that was never built. It shows "sometimes we found out that something isn't a good idea, and we don't do it."

But the building, which seems to fade into the awesome surroundings of an Enchanted Valley hemmed in by sheer cliffs, remains to face more seasons, like a scene from an Ansel Adams still life.

Its strengthened timbers will shelter rangers, hikers and horsemen from mountain storms. But most important to its friends, it will delight most of its visitors with a look at history that still lives.

WILDERNESS

OUT THE GREYWOLF VALLEY

Out the Greywolf valley
in late afternoon
after eight days in the high meadows
hungry, and out of food,
the trail broke into a choked
clearing, apples grew gone wild
hung on one low bough by a hornet's nest.
caught the drone in tall clover
lowland smell in the shadows
then picked a hard green one:
watched them swarm.
smell of the mountains still on me.
none stung.

—Gary Snyder

THE CLIFFS OF BALDY
—for Mary Belmont

This piece of lowland trail
unfolds along the Elwha
through massive fluted
pillars of old Doug fir,
and thick moss-velvet antlers
of the maple.

At one spot, the river,
like the sky
is blue, and black
branches of bank alders
engrave the snow
face of a mountain.

A winter wren
flickers through the tangle
of a wind-thrown fir,
and one solitary merganser
preens on a rock, midstream.

On the winding trail itself:
leaves of pale green lichens,
cloven tracks and snow;

and between us and the river,
elk
coming russet through the trees.

When we gain the footbridge
high on the cliffs of Baldy,
the river, broader now
and milky jade,
sweeps to sheer rock
and must go another way—

and goes.

— *Michael O'Connor*

THE RIVER TRAIL

by E. B. Webster

When I want to enjoy an outing, a real outing, when I want to forget business, to get rid of nerves, or insomnia, I hit the trail.

There is a vast difference between a trail and a road. About the latter there is a sameness, a tiresomeness; it looks very much alike, mile on mile. It is crowded with cars and trucks; sometimes dusty, again wet and slippery. On the hillside roads it often seems as though danger, even death, lies in wait just beyond every curve. Here and there, you will recall, a car plunged over; perhaps one of them contained your neighbors, your friends...

On the other hand, the trail has individuality. After one or two trips a man becomes intimate with it. He longs to return to it and enter upon it. He looks forward with pleasure to again renewing his acquaintance with each feature: the streams, the waterfalls, the rocks and cliffs, the canyons, vistas of river and mountain peaks, unusual trees, groups of flowering shrubbery; even the tiny bridges have their peculiarities. All are different.

He wonders, too, if he will again find a band of elk in this or that old-time feeding ground; if there will be deer in a certain draw; if he will again catch sight of a bear in a berry patch or on the river bar. Every bend in the trail brings pleasant memories, even if it is only of a brood of instantly vanishing valley quail.

One comes to have a feeling of companionship with a trail. To me, it matters little whether the trail leads to the home or camp of a friend on the river, to mountain parks or summits, or if it just simply trails on and on. It may be man-made; it may be an elk or a deer trail. If I become tired of the one, I know that I can always take the other.

Possibly the trail leading to the Olympic Hot Springs might be taken as a fair example. One enters the timber immediately on leaving the car at the end of the road. Fir and cedar—great old forest giants, four or five feet in diameter—make an almost complete canopy overhead, while underfoot is a delightful springy cushion of rotting wood, evergreen needles, and the fibrous roots of thimbleberry, salal, Oregon grape, huckleberry, and princess pine. Ferns—lady, deer, maidenhair, swamp, and bracken—are scattered everywhere, and great bunches of sword or Christmas fern, each frond from two to four feet in length, completely cover large areas of the forest floor. Of flowers, the evergreen yellow violet is the most numerous—immense white and pink trilliums come next, with red bleeding hearts or dialetra, pyrolas, evergreen raspberry, Scouler's bluebell, and many other species lending variety and color.

Between the flowering shrubbery and plants and the roof of the forest, two hundred feet or more overhead, lies, like a silvery cloud-drift along the mountainside, an intermediate strata of foliage—lace-like yew, plumy hemlock, the fretwork of alders, and the maple's large cool leaves, each a full twelve inches or more in diameter.

Nowhere is the trail straight; on the contrary it is continually winding in and out, around the great boles of trees or past the end of some fallen forest monarch, the while sweeping in long curves to cross a tiny stream, and again out around the point of a low ridge. Presently one comes to the base of high moss covered cliffs, dripping with fern and saxifrage and brightened with stonecrop and lilies, while in the niches are red flowering currant, red huckleberry, white dogwood and an occasional waxy syringa. Along the trail are masses of rocks which have been split by frost from the cliffs above.

All foliage is moist, fresh and bright green, quite in contrast to the dust-laden trees and fern along the roadside.

Now one comes to a slight rise at the water's edge and steps out upon a narrow bridge, hung on poles across the face of a cliff. Fifty feet below, the Elwha, apparently issuing out from the base of the mountain ridge a quarter mile distant, strikes the base of the cliff and turns at right angles, a broad band of swiftly tumbling white water. If you are lucky you may see a deer standing beneath the alders at the edge of the stream, or a pair of mergansers playing in the swirling pool at the bend.

A few yards farther, through more open timber, and the subdued music of a minor stream is heard. The trail drops a few feet to a log crossing Hughes Creek. On the right the two hundred foot rock wall of the mountain is pierced by the narrowest of canyons, down which the stream tumbles in a succession of tiny waterfalls, the source of the elusive, echoing, subdued stream-music. On the left, the stream widens, flowing through a maple-bottom, each tree of which is heavily moss-covered, the trunks enclosed in springy cushions from two to four inches in thickness. ...

Always the water appears to be boiling out the black mouth of a narrow canyon, or sweeping into the sunlit entrance to another, for the river, though it twists and turns, sometimes at right angles, maintains a northerly course.

Following a wide sweep around the end of the mountain, the trail gradually leaves the Elwha and enters the watershed of the Boulder, a small stream having many tributaries, such as Cougar and Crystal creeks, all with their sources in the snowfields and lakes of the ridges directly above.

Almost every yard of the Boulder is canyoned, as, indeed, are all Olympic mountain streams, and waterfalls by the hundreds are spaced throughout its length. Glimpses of the stream are had at intervals, always a ribbon of white in a deep green setting far down in the depths below.

Soon after rounding the mountain ridge, the character of timber changes, the trees smaller and closer-set, yet more open because of the lack of underbrush. Mountain shrubs take the place of those of the lowland, the number of pines increases, there is little fallen timber, and few flowers. Bunches of basket or elk grass with their beautiful, plume-like spikes of waxy-white flowers are frequent, while flowering dogwood, red-barked madrona and its bush-like cousin whose only name is its scientific appellation, *Arctostaphylos tomentosa*, feature the undergrowth. ...

About this time one begins to wonder how long it will be before he reaches the Olympic [Hot] Springs, with its hot baths and refreshing swimming pools, and the dinner which he well knows will be fit for the gods. All day, if he has slowly sauntered the ten mile trail, he has been enjoying the pure mountain air, laden with the perfume of flowers and the scent of balsam. But now there drifts down the trail a faint, elusive odor of an entirely different character, something like that of the ancient henfruit. Only a mere whiff at first, and for a moment he hesitates. Then another slight breeze ripples the foliage and he has it placed. The springs are not far distant now and presently he will note a thin cloud of vapor arising, for here are some twenty-odd separate springs, some hot, some hotter, and some — hot!

Hung on a narrow shelf on the mountainside, over a canyon threaded by the roaring Boulder in its express train speed to the Elwha and the sea, the hotel presently comes into view. A hundred-foot-high bridge is to be crossed before one reaches the hotel, the bath houses, the open air pools and the rows of tents and tent-houses where comfortable beds and abundant fresh air insure a night of deep, unbroken slumber.

Elwha River 1908

WHERE WATER COMES TOGETHER
WITH OTHER WATER

I love creeks and the music they make.
And rill, in glades and meadows, before
they have a chance to become creeks.
I may even love them best of all
for their secrecy. I almost forgot
to say something about the source!
Can anything be more wonderful than a spring?
But the big streams have my heart too.
And the places streams flow into rivers.
The open mouths of rivers where they join the sea.
The places where water comes together
with other water. Those places stand out
in my mind like holy places.
But those coastal rivers!
I love them the way some men love horses
or glamorous women. I have a thing
for this cold swift water.
Just looking at it makes my blood run
and my skin tingle. I could sit
and watch these rivers for hours.
Not one of them like any other.
I'm 45 years old today.
Would anyone believe it if I said
I was once 35?
My heart empty and sere at 35!
Five more years had to pass
before it began to flow again.
I'll take all the time I please this afternoon
before leaving my place alongside this river.
It pleases me, loving rivers.
Loving them all the way back
to their source.
Loving everything that increases me.

— *Raymond Carver*

from THIS HOUSE OF SKY

by Ivan Doig

A final flame-lit prism of remembering: the February afternoon at a northern Pacific coastline, Carol and I with a pair of friends hiking beside the exploding surf. Gray, restless after-storm weather, my favorite mood of the fir-shagged wild shore. In a dozen journeys here, Carol and I repeat to each other, never have we seen the waves break so high and far. After a short mile, at Ellen Creek, the four of us pause. The creek's meek tea-colored flow has boiled wide, swirly, as the ocean surf drums into the mouth of the channel and looses giant whorls of tide up the start of the stream. John, ever the boldest of us, explores a route inland, across a log to the coiling creek-bank opposite and there bushwhacking his way atop other logs and debris until he at last drops safely back to the ocean beach. I am uneasy, thinking through the chances of one of us snapping a leg in the rain-slick debris or slipping the ten-foot drop into the creek. The Ellen is a known channel that Carol and I have crossed and recrossed casually all the times before. With the storm surf nosing at it as it is, the stream may have risen now to thigh-high, but still a wader's depth. I suggest that I go across upstream of the surf line, find the shallowest route for Carol and Jean to come after; they agree. Boots slung around my neck, I slog rapidly into the water. At the deepest part the water surprises me for an instant by lapping just over my belt, then as I begin the last dozen pulling strides to the shore, a vast slosh of tide swells across the top of my chest and undertow lifts away my feet.

Like a bug down a drain I am sucked feet first into the ocean, gravel beating up at me like shrapnel as the surf plows its roaring way, shore and sky and all else lost in the water avalanche. After forever, I am reversed, surge back to the tideline, slammed down, then rolled to sea again. Now I paddle to stay upright, and simply am turned and turned, toylike, within the next acres of water until I am struck against the shore again. Taken out into the froth yet again, this time I try to ride the surf with my body, eagling my arms wide; again I am pitched over and over, hurled to gravel, instantly lifted away and out. How many times this repeats, there is no counting—perhaps as few, and as many, as five. Even as my body is being beaten limp, my mind finds incredible clarity, as if the thinking portion of me had been lifted separately and set aside from the ocean's attack. While my arms and legs automatically try trick after trick to pull me atop the water and onto the precipice of the shore, the feeling of death settles into me, bringing both surprise at the ease and calm of the process and a certain embarrassed chiding of myself that this is a silly and early method to exit from life. John later told me that, as I came whirling out of the surf one more time, he saw on my face a look of deep resignation. My remembering of that eye-locked instant is of noting him, mouth open in a shout I cannot hear, beginning to run from forty yards away, and then in my next writhe within the dense falling wall of surf, discovering his arm across my back and under me, dragging my weary three-pointed stumble from the undertow. At the shallow moving seam of shore and surf, John exults in my ear: "We've got it made now!" But I sense, as if a monstrous paw poised just beyond the edge of my vision, the next set of waves toppling toward us: we both are struck flat, but somehow hold the shore. Only then, in the wash back to sea of that aftermost wave, do my boots finally float free from around my neck, and John reaches casually as they pass and plucks them from the last of the water. Now Carol and Jean at our sides, flung to us through the flooding creek by their desperation and the luck of an interval between tidal whirlpools, their hands and John's steadying me at last, up off the cold bite of the shore gravel, I stand again.

SHI SHI

Shi Shi
   promise her
never to leave,
come back
arms full of grief.

Shi Shi
sound of silk curtains parting,
the rain-without-end
days and nights
   one body.

All night,
the spruce-needle rain on the roof.
Shi Shi
   Shi Shi...

— *Robert Sund*

MEDITATION AT OYSTER RIVER

I

Over the low, barnacled, elephant-colored rocks,
Come the first tide-ripples, moving, almost without sound, toward me,
Running along the narrow furrows of the shore, the rows of dead
                                    clam shells;
Then a runnel behind me, creeping closer,
Alive with tiny striped fish, and young crabs climbing in and out of
                                    the water.

No sound from the bay. No violence.
Even the gulls quiet on the far rocks,
Silent, in the deepening light,
Their cat-mewing over,
Their child-whimpering.

At last one long undulant ripple,
Blue-black from where I am sitting,
Makes almost a wave over a barrier of small stones,
Slapping lightly against a sunken log.
I dabble my toes in the brackish foam sliding forward,
Then retire to a rock higher up on the cliff-side.
The wind slackens, light as a moth fanning a stone:
A twilight wind, light as a child's breath
Turning not a leaf, not a ripple.
The dew revives on the beach-grass;
The salt-soaked wood of a fire crackles;
A fish raven turns on its perch (a dead tree in the rivermouth),
Its wings catching a last glint of the reflected sunlight.

II

The self persists like a dying star,
In sleep, afraid. Death's face rises afresh,
Among the shy beasts, the deer at the salt-lick,
The doe with its sloped shoulders loping across the highway,
The young snake, poised in green leaves, waiting for its fly,
The hummingbird, whirring from quince-blossom to morning-glory—
With these I would be.

And with water: the waves coming forward, without cessation,
The waves, altered by sand-bars, beds of kelp, miscellaneous
driftwood,
Topped by cross-winds, tugged at by sinuous undercurrents
The tide rustling in, sliding between the ridges of stone,
The tongues of water, creeping in, quietly.

III

In this hour,
In this first heaven of knowing,
The flesh takes on the pure poise of the spirit,
Acquires, for a time, the sandpiper's insouciance,
The hummingbird's surety, the kingfisher's cunning —
I shift on my rock, and I think:
Of the first trembling of a Michigan brook in April,
Over a lip of stone, the tiny rivulet;
And that wrist-thick cascade tumbling from a cleft rock,
Its spray holding a double rain-bow in early morning,
Small enough to be taken in, embraced, by two arms,—
Or the Tittebawasee, in the time between winter and spring,
When the ice melts along the edges of afternoon.
    And the midchannel begins cracking and heaving from the pressure
beneath,
The ice piling high against the iron-bound spiles,
Gleaming, freezing hard again, creaking at midnight —
As I long for the blast of dynamite,
The sudden sucking roar as the culvert loosens its debris of branches
and sticks,
Welter of tin cans, pails, old bird nests, a child's shoe riding a log,
As the piled ice breaks away from the battered spiles,
And the whole river begins to move forward, its bridges shaking.

IV

Now, in this waning of light,
I rock with the motion of morning;
In the cradle of all that is,
I'm lulled into half-sleep
by the lapping of water,
Cries of the sandpiper.
Water's my will, and my way,
And the spirit runs, intermittently,
In and out of the small waves,
Runs with the intrepid shorebirds—
How graceful the small before danger!

At the first of the moon,
All's a scattering,
A shining.

— *Theodore Roethke*

LOST IN THE WOODS

by Bruce Brown

It was only later that I began to reflect on the fact that "kloochman" means "wife" in Chinook jargon.

At the time, I was deep in bushwhacking bravado. Trying to hike quickly through the lush, trailless rain forest, I concentrated all my attention on ducking, jumping and constantly reassessing our course. I thought I would be safe if I could just move a little faster, but, as it turned out, this approach was the very thing that would nearly kill me before the afternoon was out.

My wife, Lane, and I lost the trail down from Kloochman Rock on the west coast of Washington state almost as soon as we descended into the forest. No longer maintained by the Olympic National Park, the trail had reverted to an informal, largely inscrutable system of blazes spray-painted on the trunks of trees.

Lane wanted to double back immediately and pick up the trail, but I was of a different mind. We had just left the splendid vista from an altitude of 3,300 feet at the top of Kloochman, and I was imbued with confidence. Goaded by the knowledge that time was short, I wanted to press on overland to our camp by the Queets River, about six miles distant. We could see the Queets twisting in the valley below, we knew in what direction we wanted to go, and traveling overland was often actually faster than trying to stay on the faint trail. So why not strike out cross-country, I argued. Actually, we didn't argue, even though we probably should have. Lane just rolled her eyes and fell behind.

We made quite good time for the first hour, romping down a long inclined ridge like skiers on a slope of powder. We were enjoying ourselves so much that I failed to notice that we had missed the trail where I had expected to hit it again. By 4:30, as the afternoon shadows began to lengthen, we entered a deep dell along the headwaters of a stream called Coal Creek. Consulting the map, and judging we were less than a mile from where the trail had to cut back again below, we decided to continue down the funneling gorge through lush growths of ferns and moss. Before long, the increasing narrowness of the gorge and the thick growth of devil's club slowed us to a crawl.

At twilight, we came to a particularly narrow and tricky section of the canyon, and here, in a blind on a small island, we found the moss-covered skeleton of a bull elk, complete with its huge antlers. I wondered how this great beast had come here to die. Had he hurled himself off the cliffs, or wandered in along the deep, twisting stream as we had done? Lane was becoming increasingly concerned about our situation. Experienced in the outdoors, she began to say aloud what she had previously let me know only with looks, namely that it was possible that we couldn't follow the creek through to its intersection with the trail. This meant we would either have to backtrack for more than an hour or (appreciable pause) go up the cliffs that now towered over us on both sides.

I was in no mood to discuss this. It seemed to me we were wasting precious time talking. We've got to keep moving, I told myself, and bulled ahead, trailing Lane's unanswered questions after me. Lane followed reluctantly. Within a few minutes I nearly joined the old elk when I leapt into a slick bowl of stream-sculptured rock, lost my footing and came within inches of plunging over a 90-foot waterfall onto boulders below. Using interlocking wrist holds, Lane was able to haul me back up to her level, where we looked deeply into each other's eyes. I said, "I'm too stupid to live." We both laughed, but more from relief than good humor. It was clear that we had an impassable path before us and an hour of daylight left to cover the distance that should take nearly an hour and a half under good conditions.

Not knowing what else to do, we climbed straight up a steep scree slope on the left side of the creek, wading through hip-deep bushes until we came—to our utter surprise—upon the old Kloochman Rock trail. Our pace picked up appreciably after this, but not nearly enough. We held council. Because I had already led us into the wilderness and nearly thrown myself over a precipice, it seemed logical to me that I should now run back to our camp in a dash against the darkness. There I would retrieve the flashlight, which—of course—was safely stowed in our tent, and return for Lane. She was dubious, but tired enough to let me try any fool thing I wanted. So we kissed, and I dashed away down the trail.

Running along in the gloaming, I had a strong impulse to pin the whole misadventure on someone else. First I tried blaming it on the Kloochman view (if it hadn't been so stunning, we would have started back sooner), then the forest-products industry (if it hadn't logged so much of the view from Kloochman, the park probably would have continued maintaining the trail) and finally even Lane (if she hadn't let me lead us into this mess, we would have had no trouble at all). Even then, though, I couldn't entirely avoid thinking about my own responsibility for the affair.

By the time I stumbled into camp, vomited from fatigue, found the flashlight and headed back, I began to realize how differently Lane and I reacted to stress and how stereotypical of the two sexes our reactions might be. Like many men, I assumed command and, when difficulties arose, simply pushed harder. I resisted reconsidering my original premises and stuck to my decisions. Meanwhile, Lane, instead of striving to save the day, relaxed to survive. I discovered her a few minutes later dozing peacefully in the soft, musk-smelling bed of a deer.

And so, in addition to the wide vista from the top, Kloochman Rock ultimately provided me with a memorable interior vista. I learned that my physical abilities were greater than I thought, but also that I might have done better if I'd never had to test them. I saw how, given a chance, the sexes can complement each other and appreciated anew what might be called wifely virtue.

Even now, when I get the bit between my teeth and want to force some issue through to some inappropriate or untimely conclusion, Lane has a way of getting my ear.

The code word is "Kloochman."

RAINFORESTS OF THE OLYMPICS
by William O. Douglas

Another hold the Olympics has on me comes from the rain forests. Of the several rain forests the one to my liking is on the Hoh River. The zone that lies in the Hoh Valley below 1000 feet is as interesting and unique as any segment of our forests the nation over.

One who comes from the ocean front passes through a spruce-cedar climax forest. This lies below the 1000-foot level and is made up of the Sitka spruce, red cedar, and western hemlock. The rain forest is farther inland. Each rain forest has a bottom carved out by a glacier. The valley is not a mile wide in places and runs on average fourteen miles in length within park boundaries. The stream gradients are very gradual. Yet in spite of this and the heavy rainfall, the valley floors—consisting of glacial till and water-deposited sands and gravel—are well drained, little standing water being in evidence even after the heaviest rain.

Sitka spruce is dominant in the rain forest, some of them 300 feet high and over ten feet in diameter. Western hemlock, which rises up to 200 feet high, comes next among the conifers, and the red cedar last. Douglas fir is here too. Douglas fir, which occasionally reaches 300 feet, is what the foresters call a pioneer species. It comes in whenever the mineral soil is bared, as after a heavy windfall or fire. Since Douglas fir cannot reproduce in shade, the western hemlock and red cedar eventually take over. That process, continued indefinitely, would eliminate the Douglas fir from the Pacific Northwest forests. Something, however, is always happening that clears the thick woods and opens them up. When that occurs, Douglas fir manages to hold its own.

The Sitka spruce dominate the rain forest today. The branches and leaves of these high trees form a roof that lets in only shafts of sunlight. The understory is big leaf maple, vine maple, devil's club. Down logs are covered with a thick carpet of mosses. Sometimes they are so completely covered by moss and so heavy with young growth that they look like a low hedge. The trees are hung with mosses, liverworts, and lichens that cover the trunks and even the crowns. These are the epiphytes that have no connection with the soil. They get their nutrients from rain water, wind-borne particles, and the decaying bark of their host. They are not parasites but rather hitchhikers of the rain forest. Underfoot are bracken and other ferns, the bead-ruby with glossy leaves, wood sorrel, wild strawberries, red huckleberries, and fragrant bed-straw. There are snails and millipedes in the moss. Some lichens are coral colored with brilliant red tips. Some are shaped like cups and painted orange.

Due to the extreme wetness of the forest, the down logs are ancient relics. Decomposition is so slow that some have lain there for 400 years. They often have tiny rows of Sitka spruce on them, seedlings not more than a few inches high. The seeds that fall on the damp ground, heavy with moss, ferns, and grass, have little chance for survival. Those that land on the old log have head room to grow and lesser competition. This old log will be a nurse to the seedlings for many years. In time they will send their roots down and around the nurse log to the ground. For some years the new trees will appear to be standing on stilts. But in time—perhaps several hundred years later—the nurse log will have decomposed, much of it being absorbed by the new trees. Then the roots will enlarge and fill up the space left by the nurse log. Those that travel the forest on that future day will see giants where I saw seedlings. Not knowing about the old nurse log, they may wonder why it is that these new trees are swollen, distorted, and heavily buttressed at the base. And they may also wonder why the trees stand in a row, giving a colonnade effect.

Loggers often claim that overage trees and down trees are wasted and should be removed. That is a false premise in the Olympics. For in the true rain forest these rotting logs are the best seed ground available.

Thanks to elk, the forest floor is fairly free of thick underbrush; one can see for some distance.

On a rainy day the force of the storm is broken by the treetops. Only a slight drizzle comes through. After a hard rain the trees will drip for days. On a bright day the shafts of sunlight fill the rain forest with a soft green light that is restful to the eyes. Rain or shine, this forest has a quiet that is deep and profound. A winter wren sings high overhead. Though few birds are seen in the rain forest, many breed there—ruffled grouse, jays, tanagers, grosbeaks, finches, siskins, juncos, warblers, and song sparrows. A snow-shoe rabbit runs underfoot. A Douglas squirrel sounds the alarm. Every noise is soft and muted. The quiet and the light induce a mood of reverence. This is not the place to run, to shout. This is a cathedral, draped in mosses and lichens and made of gigantic trees. The trees alone are enough to bring humility to man. The western hemlock is over twenty-five feet in girth, Douglas fir over fifty feet, and Sitka spruce over forty feet. These are virgin trees in a virgin forest. They would have disappeared by now if the logging interests had had their way. There are some who see in them no more than so many board feet. But they are among the great wonders of creation. Kellogg bluegrass and delicate trefoil foam flower flourish near the trail in the rain forest. The trailing raspberry with its starry five-petaled white flowers is bright. The showy miner's lettuce, with white petals, makes a thick stand. The waxen white wintergreen and rose-colored Oregon oxalis sorrel are almost hidden in the litter of the forest floor. The snowberry—later to have a white fruit—shows pink flowers. Everywhere stands the graceful vanilla leaf, its slender cluster of white flowers high on a single stem rising above one leaf divided into three broad leaflets.

There are fungi in every forest and every field. But I never feel their presence so vividly as I do in the rain forest. Here are molds, mildew, mushrooms, shelf fungus, rust, to mention only a few. Thousands of others work unseen in the vegetation that makes a soft, thick carpet underfoot. Some produce spores that fill the air and cause people to suffer from allergies. But all of them perform functions crucially essential to forests and fields.

Forest humus is not a mass of plant remains but a living mass of fungi. The genera alone run into the thousands. Bacteria predominate in soil rich in nutrients, cultivated, and fertilized. Fungi are more active in the forests and in compact, poor soils. They are present even in nearly pure salicious sands.

Since the fungi have no chlorophyll, they lack the means of manufacturing their own food. They must, therefore, be parasites and live on other living things, or be saprophytes, or scavengers, and live on dead organic matter. They do one or the other, most of them being saprophytic. The latter have a far wider range of food than the parasites.

Parasites do not live on vegetation alone. Some live on microscopic animals, insects, worms, fluke eggs, and the larvae of mosquitoes.

While some saprophytes are scavengers of vegetable matter, others consume the carcasses of animals, some live on animal excrement, and so on. Each supply of organic material seems to have its special saprophyte.

Dozens of strains of fungi have been shown to be capable of inhibiting the growth of bacteria and of producing a variety of antibiotic substances. Some fungi destroy other fungi that are parasitic, and bacteria as well.

Soil-inhabiting fungi produce organic acids which dissolve inorganic soil elements such as calcium, magnesium, and phosphorus and make them available for food. Sometimes this food, produced by the fungi, is used by them. Most of it, however, is used by green plants. The decomposed materials, not eaten by the fungi or used by the green plants, are left as humus. Humus is resistant to rapid attack by micro-organisms and forms a cohesive part of the soil system. These soil fungi—whether in forests or fields—are, therefore, highly important to soil fertility.

The logs at my feet in the Olympics have been collecting spores of fungi from the time the trees fell. Only those spores which can use this particular wood will flourish on this down timber. Some fungi feed on hardwoods, some on conifers, some on leaves. Each has its special diet. One set of fungi may cause the primary decay in the logs; another set may come in later and attack the remains. Some fungi, such as the coral mushroom, are parasitic on the roots of trees. Poking my foot into the litter of the forest floor, I turn up a small colony of mushrooms, *Agaricus subrutilescens*. These tender morsels, low to the ground and shaped like a Japanese parasol, are delicious when broiled in butter. They are one of many mushrooms that flourish in the dark, damp wood of the rain forest. And when we pick them it has no more effect on the mushroom plant than picking fruit from a tree. What we pick is the fruit. The plant is a vast network of threads so fine that they are not visible to the naked eye until they are twisted into strands. These threads produce enzymes which digest food particles outside the threads. When the digested material is in solution, and only then, is it absorbed by the plant. The spores of this dainty mushroom at my feet will spread; but the plant will produce mushrooms over and again. If I can only mark this spot, I will find, on my return after more warm rains, a new crop from the old plant.

I learned in the Olympics an important lesson in ecology. The lesson is that wilderness areas are essential to our long-time welfare and well-being as a nation. The wilderness area is the norm. In the areas where man has introduced crops, sprays, fertilizers, the ecological balance has been upset.

At times the result may be harmful. DDT can make milk from cows dangerous to humans. Certain fruit sprays kill bees that are essential to pollenization. At other times the remedy used by man merely helps nature in her corrective process. Yet the wilderness stands as the true "control" plot for all experimentation in the animal and vegetable worlds. Only through knowledge of the norm can an appraisal of the abnormal or diseased be made. The "control" plot, where vegetable and animal growth continues undisturbed, is as essential to successful diagnosis and management of soil conditions as normal individuals are to the practice of medicine.

That is, I think, what Thoreau meant when he wrote, "In wilderness is the preservation of the world." Farming, for example, imports plants, animals, and fertilizers. It eliminates native flora and fauna and even some of the unseen fungi and bacteria that have built the soil. All this is necessary for human existence. But will it stabilize the soil or will we end up with sterile land and ugly gullies? No one knows. Nature got stability by encouraging great diversity. We do not yet know whether we can do the same through man-made substitutes.

No species should ever be eliminated, for man in his wisdom does not yet know the full wonders and details of the cosmic scheme.

On one side lichens, fungi, insects, bacteria, mammals, birds, and on the other the trees, ferns, and underbrush are interlocked or combined into a community in this Olympic forest. It is a community of competition and of interdependence. It is a series of food chains too intricate for man to comprehend in all its ramifications.

The rain forests are so radiant with soft green light, so filled with endless wonders that I hate to leave them.

THE PUNCHEON TRAIL

Between wild hedges, green and tall,
Of huckleberry, fern and brake,
Salal and salmon-berry bush,
Lifting its fruit for you to take,
Oregon grape, its glossy leaves
Catching the light of passing day,
All growing rank on either side—
The Forks-Spruce trail took up its way.

And where the ground was wet and low,
Was hazardous with holes and bogs,
The trail was laid along the top,
With stringers, and with half-split logs;
And when the sun could reach within
The heavy growth which stood in ranks,
All beauty lay upon the scene,
Shadow, and light, and thick green banks.

But when the sky was dark with rain
The puncheon trail lay like a snare,
All slimy-wet, and treacherous,
Catching me stumbling, unaware.
I slipped along, and as I went,
It was as though I'd lost a friend;
Was this my sun-kissed thoroughfare?
This sullen byway, without end—

The clatter as of a thousand hoofs,
Against the wooden surface pounds,
Crowding each other as they come,
A herd of baby elk now bounds
From out the woods; their tufted heads
Held high; alert their eager eyes,
They thunder down the puncheon trail,
And leave me there—in paradise.

— *Dolly Stearns Harman*

GRAY FLAGS OF THE HILLS

Olympics, Olympics, moist home of the mists,
How sure do thy signals, thy flags on the hills,
Call troops of cloud soldiers through tortuous twists
To plunge where a trumpet each cataract thrills.
　　　　　Each cataract thrills,
　　　　　Thy thousand new rills
　　　　　Wild trumpets of rivers,—
　　　　　Gray flags of the hills!

Olympics, Olympics, thy fortress of fir,
Thy cavernous hemlocks where world clamor stills,
Where never an elk hears the arrow's weird whirr,
A wilderness peace till the fierce cougar kills.
　　　　　The fierce cougar kills,
　　　　　His blood lust fulfills,
　　　　　Thy shroud for the timid,—
　　　　　Gray flags of the hills!

Olympics, Olympics, thy swift waters run
To grind the huge boulders in rough granite mills,
A smile at the labor, a kiss from the sun,
They dance as they whirl their rude hammers and drills.
　　　　　Rude hammers or drills,
　　　　　As glad worker wills;
　　　　　Thy rivers are laughing,—
　　　　　Gray flags of the hills!

— *Edmond S. Meany*

ELK ON THE ELWHA

Everyone's going all the way in poems:
you and I in bed, naked against each other.
My eyes wander your belly's innocent curves,
taking up the trail of dark hairs,
descending inexorably to the wild—

but think of it, that day
they surprised us, one of them thirty feet ahead,
crossing our trail in the November dusk.
We stopped and she stared and we stared,
and then she crossed, behind her, the herd,
cows and leggy summer calves, elk
we had wanted to see for years.

Their camel rumps startled us in the green,
and thick, unmistakable,
their wild scent mastered for those moments
the air. In *their* version,
we surprised them, and they were quick to melt
into the northwest brush, old dead logs
or devil's club stripped of leaves. Their high shrill—
eerie in an animal big as a horse—
came twenty minutes later, from the river,
calling the herd together.

That afternoon, looking for them, we'd already flushed
two buck, white tails, and later, in the glasses,
found three huge bulls camouflaged
in the gold of fallen bigleaf maple leaves—
lost them again in a breath.
Elusive, safe, like these poems of bodies and love.
We lose ourselves in what happens.

After we'd given up looking, we came out
to the river, past the rotting cabin
called Hume's Ranch, past the meadow
filled with their droppings, our course set
for the bridge over the first big rapids.

Up there, on the bluff, it's all maple.
Around us, piles of goldleaf, above us,
the huge trees stripped to their naked, mossed limbs,
and out on the river flats, cottonwoods, still in leaf,
yellow torches along the milk-blue Elwha.

How do the elk manage that liquid step
the deer have when they leap—all power, no noise?
Why is it when the light begins to fail,
the luminosity of a fall day emerges
in the cold? We walked, single file,
unaware, your blue trail jacket threading its way
through darkening air.

— *Alice Derry*

NIGHT AT THREE FORKS SHELTER

A rosary of maidenhair
in black soil—Jesus, do I mumble.
On the floor of roots
needles flake against my boot.
Boulders scrape and whisper
in the silt; their voices woke me.
Faces of trillium
rose over the trail.
A moth touched my nose
and I stumbled into sweet mold,
my hand sinking in the moss,
mushrooms cold on my cheek.
Forget it, no voice is calling.
I'm a stone in a shadow.
Cameron, Grand & Graywolf
cut through rock and sound.
This is easy: I write them down.
No one believes I make them meet.

— *Michael Daley*

NATURALLY DRAWN

Mountains never seem lonely. They lean
into each other, companionable, the contours
ascending rhythmically
or falling away to the plains.

Here I am with an hour to myself by the mudflats.
The summer's long overcast has pushed back to sun.
Sandpipers walk on their shadows in the water-shine.
I sing to myself quietly as beach grass.

This is the season of ants and poppies. Seed pods
on High Divide rattle the passing of hikers.
I too take the warmth to my body. Soon
I'll be with you, sharing these small adventures.

— *Charlotte Warren*

TREES OF THE TIMBERLINE
by E. B. Webster

There is so much to be seen from a mountain ridge; the view, whichever way one may turn, is so wonderful; the immediate pinnacles and cliffs are so impressive, and the flowers so beautiful that one fails, in two or three trips, to get anything more than a general idea of the mountains and the scenery beyond. Not until one has made several visits, does he begin to note the really interesting things which Nature has strewn all along his pathway. ...

One of the most interesting features of the mountain ridges is what is known as "timber line," or, rather, the character of the trees at timber line. Here, where terrific winds sweep, where snow comes early and piles up until it has tremendous crushing force, where it freezes nearly every night during the short season of growth, all trees are stunted and nearly all misshapen. Their trunks are abnormally thickened, a twisted mass of knots, the wood as dense and hard as the "hard woods" of the eastern states, their basal limbs longer, much longer, than the height of the tree, and their tops mere spikes.

Trees which grow in the shelter of the rock-encircled parks, or behind a pinnacle where they are not buffeted by the prevailing winds, are more normal, though short and stocky; often they make a very respectable dense forest. But those which have to contend with the elements are universally deformed.

There are trees on Mt. Angeles not twenty feet in height with trunks three feet in diameter. There are living trees two feet in diameter, every foot of the trunk lying prone on the ground, having basal limbs fifteen and even twenty feet in length—limbs stocky, thickly branched and densely covered with needles. In a particularly windswept location, where a number of trees have started life together, their branches will be so matted that one can literally walk on top, without paying any particular attention to the placing of his feet, and with absolutely no possibility of stepping through to the ground; one notable example of such stunted and matted forest is found on the south side of the Third Peak.

All trees in windswept locations have limbs only on one side, that away from the wind. Either the limbs which start on the windward side are broken off before they attain any size and strength, or they are gradually bent around into streamers in line with the prevailing winds. Thus in the Olympics, where the southwest and northwest trades are the prevailing winds, all limbs trend easterly. A compass is absolutely unnecessary on a mountain top, even in the densest fog. ...

Surely this, and a thousand other similar things in the mountains, are remarkable, worthy the study of anyone interested in the out-of-doors. Yet, as I said in the beginning, such a tree is merely a seedling, and nothing more, and all things are similarly a closed book to him who thinks he knows the mountains because he has taken two or three trips to the High Places.

Two species of alpine trees always attract attention. One, the alpine fir, because of the smooth blue-black cones that stand like little owls close up alongside the trunk, the top limbs bearing them being less than a foot in length. Only this past summer I directed a friend's attention to four little owls perched on the topmost boughs of one of these trees and he looked several seconds before he burst out with "Those aren't owls!" The other is the Alaskan cedar, a tree quite different from the cedar of the low lands and having a very dense and beautiful yellow wood. Then there is the mountain ash, which grows in profusion in sheltered places; and the blue-berried or coned juniper which takes the form of a matted vine, rather than an upright bush; also the willow, two inches high, yet bearing perfect catkins one inch in length. Pines are plentiful, but only below timber line. Of the bushes, the most abundant are the white rhododendron, each being covered with hundreds of flowers; the pachistima, which is something like the familiar box of our gardens; the short alpine huckleberry and the still smaller blueberry; the red-berried kinnikinnick and the heathers, red and white.

THE ALPINE FLOWER GARDENS
by E. B. Webster

Although the glaciers with their beautifully crevassed cascades undoubt-edly constitute the greatest attraction of the Olympics—there being a greater glacial area than exists in Glacier National Park—yet Mt. Angeles has its own features of scarcely secondary interest. In fact, the very absence of the glaciers, which once filled the narrow valleys almost rim-full, is responsible for the high-stepped walls of the peaks themselves, Mt. Ange-les having more unscalable precipices than any other peak in the Olympics.

Time was when the continent was covered with glacial ice, only the tops of the mountain peaks appearing above the ice-plain. The one-time thick-ness and extent of this ice cap, so the geologists tell us, is determined by the area covered with granite boulders which were brought down, imbedded in the ice, from the far north. This ice cap, which gouged out Puget Sound and the Strait of Juan de Fuca, filled the Olympic mountain valleys, even to the headwaters of the streams. Elwha Basin is almost a solid mass of boulders, covered, in part, with a thin layer of soil from the disintegration of the ridges above. This ice cap reached about half way up the side of Mt. Angeles; in fact, just below the Half-way Rock the last large boulder is to be seen; beyond that elevation it is impossible to find a piece of granite.

During this long period of time the mountain peaks acquired a flora identical in some respects, similar in others, to that of Alaska and Siberia. Many of our Alpine plants bear Russian names, having been first collected by Russian botanists, at Alaskan trading posts.

In the course of time, as the ice receded, there was left on these peaks three distinct zones of plants. The true alpine flowers, acclimated at an ele-vation of 7,000 feet, but not to be found much below that elevation; another zone, between six and seven thousand, of plants less depauperated; and another, between four and six thousand, of sub-alpine plants. In all the many thousands of years that have passed since that time, these alpine plants have not become acclimated below their zones; neither have the sub-alpine plants been able to exist above their level.

On the high mountains, where the only soil surface is that to be found in tiny crevices in the rock pinnacles, a hundred feet high or thereabout, al-pine flowers are necessarily very limited, both in number and in species. In this strictly alpine region, the rock crests of the mountain ridges, we find bluebells, in themselves an inch across, borne by plants scarcely half an inch in height; so also there are pinks, primroses, and many others, the plants apparently little more than thin patches of moss, yet covered with flowers, disproportionately large and of intense hues.

On Mt. Angeles, where the usual fields of snow and ice are absent, their place being taken by alpine parks, there are meadows, watered by tiny streams, dotted with clumps of dwarfed alpine fir and Alaska cedar, and covered with short grass in which are growing thousands upon thousands of flowers. One may easily pick over twenty-five species in a spot less than ten yards across, or over a hundred species in a walk of a thousand feet.

Again, below these alpine parks, are the sub-alpine parks, at the head of the branches of Morse Creek and Little River—meadows at an elevation of 4,000 feet where the grass grows knee-high. Swampy in character, these have a flora all their own—lusty plants of many blossoms, red and orange and blue, all the colors of the rainbow. ...

But the real flower fields—not as regards the number nor the rarity of individual species, but in respect to the multitudes of flowers of comparatively few kinds—are the grass ridges and southern mountain slopes. These run from Mt. Constance on Hood Canal to Hurricane Hill on the Elwha, and beyond to Crystal, Happy Lake and the other ridges, nearly sixty miles of grass ridges—the Paradise Park country of the Olympics.

For the most part too low for the white heather and the host of alpine plants, as well as being too high for those of the sub-alpine meadows, their flora is limited to great fields of red heather, of blue lupines, of painted cups, bunch flowers, white cowslips, avalanche lilies both white and yellow, blue gentian, elk or basket grass, and others similar. In the thousands of acres of this park-like country the Olympics have as extensive floral fields as are to be found on the slopes of Rainier or any other mountain.

And the beauty of the Mt. Angeles country, over that which is covered with snow and ice, lies in the fact that here one may camp, not on a bench on the side of the mountain, like Paradise Park, not deep down in a sub-alpine valley, like the Elwha Basin, but way up in the High Places—between the peaks, in a true alpine garden. No other place in the whole of the Northwest, unless it may be Mt. Constance, presents an equal opportunity.

To reach the summit of a snow-clad mountain is a matter of some considerable effort, to say the least, and after spending an hour or so on the top one must return to the valley to camp. One cannot see the sun set because he is away down in the valley; one cannot see the moon rise, for he is virtually at the bottom of a well; one can see little save the timber and rocks of the ridges immediately about unless he daily undertakes the climb up those rock ridges to the summit. One is not in an alpine country, but betwixt and between.

E.B. Webster

On Angeles one may see the sun sink into the Pacific, beyond Tatoosh Island, while its last rays tint with gold and rose and purple the hundreds of snow peaks in the Olympics and Cascades. One may see the moon rise, should he be so fortunate as to be on the mountain when that orb is in its full glory, flooding every peak and rock and tree with its silvery light, and be brought to realize then, as never before, the full import of what it is to FEEL the majesty, the nobility, the strength of the hills.

OLYMPIC FLORA

Sword-fern

Many plants seem common.
Some remain wonderful
despite all of this.

    Willow

    Small velvet catkins
    make themselves available,
    mate in March wind.

        Salmonberry

        Hanging in mid air
        the closest you'll ever come
        to skeins of fish eggs.

            Flett's Violet

            Rooted so deep in scree,
            the little bit that shows
             seems extra precious.

Oxalis

As evening gathers,
three leaves fold against each stem.
Flower buds doze off.

Salal

Though it is muddy,
this trail could lead to heaven
between your broad leaves.

Elderberry

Just once a year,
when the fruit glows brilliant red,
a band-tailed pigeon comes.

Piper's Bellflower

The entire sky
leans in all directions
trying to match your blue.

— *Edward Tisch*

A FEW FROM THE OLYMPICS

Mountains filling valleys
with shadows of mountains.
Sun rolling in infinity.

Another day of fog.
Mountains hidden from view.
The slugs ecstatic.

Kneeling to wash;
on the other side
a bear.
   —Hoh River

Visiting the creek
after the storm.
Our footprints the only ones.
   —Wolf Creek

Stream and hummingbird
are my breakfast music
—this still summer day.

The day's weariness wiped away
by a single leap
into a snow-melt lake.
   —Seven Lakes Basin

This land so rich
I could even learn
to love the mosquitoes.

— Steve Sanfield

THE OLYMPIC BACKCOUNTRY
IS SLEEPING SAFE IN SNOW

by Phyllis Miletich

Some weeks ago, before any sign of snow, we drove to the top of Deer Park. It was a last chance to put the mountain to sleep. Alone up there, a whining wind bit through our clothes, whistled a soft warning. Moisture-swollen clouds pushed up the river valleys—sliding, urgent—crowding between pointed peaks. Clearly, we were intruders, come too late. Clearly, we were spies on the sacred solitude of winter's first edge. Very soon, the ancient secret ritual would begin: The closing of the High Country with snow.

Winter protects the back country from the impact of man—shuts him out and declares the invincibility of wilderness. So, I look up there and know that the mountains are resting now, put to sleep under a quilt of snow.

When the snow moves lower on the foothills, then dumps into the river valleys and finally into our back yards, the image of the Smith Ranch cabin drifts into my head. The pioneer Smith Ranch is six trail miles up the Queets River, from where you start walking at the end of the Queets Road. Only the most persistent fishermen get there—in summer, when the water's low. The thick, pushing Queets blocks the way of any casual angler. Before you'll fish near Smith Ranch, you will wade the width of the Queets, crossing it twice, and that stops a lot of them. Then you'll walk six miles in sopping boots until, finally, you'll come to where an old pioneer, standing in a dense spruce and maple bottom, decided to dig in even deeper.

Every year when snow comes and a freezing wind whistles around my house, I see that standpipe spigot just outsde Smith Cabin. No matter how tight you twisted, it always dripped—lazy fat drops, steady, hypnotic. In the solitude of winter, I see it, as dropping temperatures clamp in, squeezing these drops slower and slower and then to a stop. Once more, the backcountry is alone.

I'm not the only one with memories of favorite shelters, some of them destroyed now by federal order about nine years ago. But the order was finally rescinded, before they were all destroyed. And memories of them are indestructible. Listen to an old-timer: "Say, wouldn't it be somethin' if you and me wuz right now up at Reiman's cabin, or Sourdough Shelter, or the one in there at Diamond Meadows? We useta take the horses up over Anderson Pass and down into Enchánted Valley. Good shelters at most of them places and, by God, you'd think you wuz warm, wouldn't ya' even with one side out of the damn things and wind blowin' through the cracks? But that's a palace, ain't it, when you're tired and wet as hell?" The old-timer chuckled, remembering. "And that coffee—best coffee you ever drank."

The easy, warm talk passes back and forth; the plain good memories of coffee and bedrolls and shelters, of passes crossed, and packs shouldered, and rivers fished. Things that stick in a man's head so that he sees more, when he looks up at mountains, than other men see.

"Yep, if I ever get back into the mountains," the old-timer dreamed, "I'd like to be up at that Anderson Pass shelter. Oh God, I can remember some nice things—well, they mighta been hell, but you thought they wuz nice. And honest—it was beautiful, afterwards. You think about it then."

Four thousand miles away in New York City, there's a 35-year-old research scientist reaching for cold coffee on the sterilizer beside him. It's after midnight. Alone, he walks to the window and stares down at the sluggish Hudson, tortured and chained between sullen smokestacks and concrete towers.

Closing his eyes against the sight, he sees instead the broad, clear spread of the Hoh River, sliding free to the ocean. Or on winter nights he remembers the Skyline Trail and sees the old shelter up there, standing solitary in the glistening night; an ice-slit moon gleams on its rough roof, its hard sides a cube of sanctuary against glacier winds. And once more, a prisoner in a pulsating city is comforted by his Peninsula memories, sheltered by our wilderness.

For years the wilderness crouching at our back door has comforted city-weary pilgrims who come to plug onto our treasure. If only for a little while. With their eyes, they steal a little of that treasure and it shelters them. For in the primal memory, sunken deep like a fishhook in the brain, is caught a dream we all reach for. It may be that man keeps rendezvous with that dream, when he sits crouched on a tree stump, in a small circle of firelight, near a three-sided shelter—secure for a while in a heart's place that lets him come home.

Yes, summer will come again. And the dream-seekers will again come with it. But, now, in winter, we are the keepers of the treasure. Shhhhhh... the Olympic Backcountry is safe and sleeping. In snow.

— Port Angeles Daily News

MEDITATION ABOVE OZETTE

From the swamplands
   down in the draw
All the frogs
   you could ever hope to know
Are singing to each other.

For miles the low hills
   bow deeply to the lake
Who holds now the passing
   shadows of clouds
As one holds a promise.

East, the ridges still deep in snow are
   glowing some
And beyond them
   the last ragged patterns of geese
Have disappeared

Laughing their curious laugh
   against the night.
I try this poem once, for measure.

No one but the wind.

— Tim McNulty

MEMOIRS

HUMES RANCH: ON THE ELWHA RIVER

by Ruby El Hult

After supper, as the Crislers called the evening meal, I helped Lois do the dishes. The log cabin seemed hot and stuffy, and I was glad when I could hurry outside into the cooler air. I found Herb sitting on the porch edge with a fishpole across his lap. "How would you like trout for breakfast?" he asked as he attached a hook and leader to the fishline.

"A ridiculous question! Who wouldn't want a trout for breakfast?"

"Fishing is still pretty good on the Elwha," he said, "but not like it was when we first moved up here. In those days I used to go around to all our guests and ask how many trout of exactly what length they could eat for breakfast. I'd get up early, go down to the river, and anything I caught that didn't fit the required sizes I'd throw back. At breakfast time I would fry up exactly the right number of trout of exactly the right size. Now I take orders only by number. How many fish can you eat?"

"Oh, one or two, I suppose."

"Well, come fishing with me and see how it's done."

I ran down to fetch a sweater and caught up with Herb as he headed down a trail which began near the berry enclosure and descended steeply along the bench edge.

We crossed the spring green of what had once been Grant Humes' hayfield, and passed under a canopy of a broadleaved maple grove. The high leafy tops kept out all but a splintering of light and sunshine. Beneath the trees the ground was smoothly parklike, spread with pale green grass and a carpeting of the small, winsome, pinkish-white flowers called spring beauties.

All day I had longed to get close to this river of rush and roar, and it was wonderful when on the far edge of the maple grove we reached its low bank. Fed from snow-melt in the high peaks, the river water was more glacially pearl-gray and swirled along at a dizzier rate and with a louder din than I had expected. In its swift course it struck midstream boulders, where it leaped into the air and churned up a spray, damp and penetrating.

Herb eased himself gingerly out to the end of a soft sandbar, cast his line and became intent upon his fishing. This left me to explore the shoreline, watch trailing grasses waving their ends in the current of little eddies. The sun moved up the opposite mountainside, leaving the Elwha bottoms in shadow. I felt the chill of the evening and the misty river spray seeping through my sweater. To keep warm I decided to walk upstream to a rustic bridge standing before a huge rock-wall barrier.

I saw that a trail, which followed the upper edge of the field, crossed the river by way of the rustic bridge and disappeared into the brush and trees opposite.

I ventured out on the bridge and in the upstream direction was confronted by the wildest and most tumultuous scene imaginable. The rock cliffs proved to be the downstream end of a constricting canyon. For as far up the river's course as I could see, this canyon kept the waters in heaped-up confinement, where they churned, boiled, turned turtle, fumed, foamed and leaped like insane dancers up and down the canyon walls, all with the mighty clamor of a freight-train station. The narrow little bridge crossed where the channel widened and the river, as with vast relief, spread out to a more normal course. But its waters kept their force and momentum as far down the valley as I could follow their antics.

The experience was exhilarating. First I would lean on one pole railing and watch the mad gyrations of the pent-up waters in the canyon and admire the filmy ferns and dainty flowers growing on the mossy rock walls. I would then lean on the other railing and grow giddy watching the down-stream rush. On his sandbar I saw Herb reel in a wriggling, silvery fish.

Presently Herb came up and joined me on the bridge, proudly display-ing four trout hung on a willow branch. We stood side by side observing the water-battle in the upstream canyon. "The Grand Canyon of the Elwha," he shouted in my ear. "Impassable stretch—six miles."

I thought of the Press Party, those hardy Olympic explorers, who had been told by the lying mayor of Port Angeles that the Elwha River was navigable for thirty miles into the mountains. In the miserable weather of midwinter they built a little bastard boat, the Gertie, imbibing "medicinal whiskey" for sore thumbs, freezing toes and frustration.

The boat started upriver on January 13, 1890, but the Elwha River was not as promised. The current was swift, with rapids, shallows, boulders, tree sweepers and piles of driftwood barring the way. The Gertie was only an encumbrance, and after a half-dozen miles of dragging her forward foot by foot, the men abandoned her. I wished they had got her this far upstream. One look at this wild canyon and they would have despaired and left the Gertie in the bushes and I could go searching for her last remains.

Herb and Lois Crisler

CARETAKER

It is an awesome task,
the dream of a boy
who pressed leaves
between pages,
a young man who taught me
the Latin names of species.
I still remember Acer rubrum.
You are called
superintendent, bureaucrat,
and more.

At Rialto, I play tag with the surf,
you roll pebbles in your hand,
issues in your head:
Soleduck Road, Elwha Dams...
my voice brings you back.
We watch the sea inhale,
draw back, crackle over stone.
Clouds, your thoughts, drift.
You look past the horizon
away from the time
that was to be
ours.

Even now, we hold hands
our special way, stop to embrace,
plan our future—though briefer
than before.
We balance on a tangle of beached logs,
test limits as we did in our youth.
Fog rolls in and you, with longer legs,
leaner form, disappear in its white haze.

Smaller, smaller,
until you are a blue-eyed boy
with crackers, a can of beans
in your pocket.
We are on our way
to Ft. Washington or Harper's Ferry
before they were national monuments.
Me, naive to the way of woods,
suggested we walk to the end
of a path on a day's outing.
You, with a secret, know
it to be the Appalachian Trail.
I still delight in that daffy grin.

I recall
when we swam the inlet
to Assateague Island,
the current pulling us seaward.
Dizzy with fatigue,
aware we'd been foolish,
we walked through a perfect day.
A herd of wild horses
thundered through dune grass.
We stood dazzled,
felt their vibration long after
they were gone.
A pristine island, a girl and boy
alone, carefree.

Caretaker,
it is not the same.
For now, this Gem
is yours to protect, preserve.
Let's go back,
climb a pinnacle,
sit on a craggy throne.

— *Mitzi Chandler*

PACK TRAIN GRANDMA
by Marian Taylor

"Grandma, did you really own a little bear?" asked Danielle.

"Could you really ride a horse and shoot a gun?" asked Lindsay.

My two granddaughters and I were looking at some of my old mountain pictures. When I answered yes, the two little girls were excited and quite impressed.

"Tell us about it and how come you had a bear anyway," they asked. So here's the story.

When I was fourteen my mother married Frank Vincent, veteran guide and packer in the Olympics. His territory was the Dosewallips River country. Why me instead of my brother when he picked a helper? I'm not sure that I definitely was the more interested. At the age of ten I had been given a copy of *Tarzan of the Apes* for Christmas and from that time had tried to emulate him. I didn't want to be Jane, I wanted to be like Tarzan. Many a young fir tree bore wounds caused by my efforts to swing from limb to limb. No matter that Washington firs were not made for swinging, I tried. Perhaps I had succeeded to some extent and perhaps Frank saw Tarzan in me and made his choice.

Frank taught me to ride and shoot and throw a diamond hitch over a loaded packhorse. An affinity developed between the horses and me. The Dosewallips was Frank's country and soon became mine too.

In the spring and summer we packed in supplies for the Forest Service, back-to-nature folks, artists, photographers, botanists, sightseers and an occasional prospector. In the fall we packed in hunters and brought out their game. I was going to high school at this time but was allowed to take the hunting season off. Some of the boys griped about this but Mr. Davis told them that when they "got straight A's as Marian does" they could have the hunting season off, too.

The first trip up in the spring was hard work but exciting. In places the trail was washed out from the winter snows. Forest Service lines were down and trees were across the trail. Worst of all were the yellow-jackets who had built their nests in the muddy trail. A yellow-jacket at any time is not a friendly creature, but when a dozen or so horses have walked over their homes, they came out stinging. I always rode the last horse in the string to keep any stragglers moving. Often I rode Carrots, a rugged individualist. Where the other horses would take off bucking and kicking, Carrots would stop still in the trail and try to bite the yellow devils that were in his fetlocks. After about two such incidents I learned to hold Carrots back until the other horses had gone through, then away we went in a mad gallop, risking decapitation from dangling telephone wires.

On this first trip we usually packed in Forest Service supplies, fixed the trail, took out the fallen trees and, in some instances, were able to fix the telephone line which was a single wire attached to trees. Frank had a sort of gentleman's agreement with the rangers. When we were on the trail, we would report any potential trouble spots that we could not take care of. If

Marian Taylor

it was clear, they were saved an unnecessary long hike. In return they would let us know if the game warden was on the prowl. It had been understood for a long time that Frank could have "camp meat," but there had been a disagreement with the current game warden. The privilege had been withdrawn and now there was a sort of a contest between the two. We were always at risk.

Once as we were packing out, the ranger called and told us that the game warden was waiting at Corrigenda and that he was planning us no good. We did have camp meat and Frank had no intention of leaving it behind to spoil. Besides, he could not ignore the challenge. A mile above Corrigenda, Frank took the meat off the horse and draped it over my arm, then threw my jacket over the meat. When we got to the ranger station, the warden was waiting and carefully searched every pack. He was almost apoplectic when he found nothing and Frank thanked him for unpacking the horses for us. We went safely on our way but I had a sore arm for days from the weight of the venison.

Frank was always sure I could do anything he wanted me to. No horse ever had been ridden to the top of Mount Sentinel, so I rode Badger, Frank's saddle horse, to the top of Mount Sentinel. No horse had ever been ridden down the steep slope of Hayden, so I rode my horse, Nazimova, down the slope. One hunting season Frank walked me five miles down the trail from Camp Marian, up the mountains where we hunted all day, then back up the trail to camp again where I cooked supper for the hunting party even though it was only tomato soup. I was so tired I didn't even clean my rifle, a cardinal sin. The buck I killed that day, the last day of the hunting season, outweighed the prize-winning buck at Piper and Taft's in Seattle, but we could not get it there in time for the weighing.

We packed in many interesting people. Among them was the well-known photographer who wanted me to pose nude as an Indian maid on a rock in the river. Who me? No way!

The person I will never forget was a lawyer from Seattle who was responsible for one of our few tragedies on the trail, and one of my ugliest jobs with the pack train. Hardtack was our most temperamental horse. A big, raw-boned bay, he never really wanted to be a packhorse. He even had been seen cavorting with an elk herd one moonlit night in Dose Meadows. Once he tried to bull his way under a partly fallen tree on the trail. He happened to be carrying two large boxes of dynamite for the Forest Service at the time.

Back to the lawyer. We met him almost completely exhausted on the trail. Frank, in an unfortunately generous mood offered to put his pack on Hardtack. Hardtack already had a large crosscut saw looped to the top of his pack with the wooden handles tied together. When we got to the Dose Meadows Ranger Station, the man was eager to get his pack, but he was told he'd have to wait a few minutes until Frank or Jerry could get it for him. We were busy with our horses and did not see him disregard our orders and try to get his pack. Inadvertently he loosed one end of the saw which began to whip around violently, almost taking off his head and that of Jerry who was next to him. Hardtack, terrified, began running and bucking down the trail. With every jump the big saw was cutting into his legs and flanks. We finally caught him and Frank dressed his wounds as best he could. We had commitments and had to continue over the pass and down the Elwha. We were gone several days and the weather was hot. When we finally got back to Dose Meadows, Hardtack had been dead for several days and was in an advanced stage of decomposition. It was impossible to bury the big horse in one piece. Jerry had continued down the Elwha so there was only Frank and me. Frank had a large cut on his hand which he had received while trying to catch Hardtack, so the danger of infection was too great for him to risk doing the job. I was the one who had to cut up Hardtack. As I said, I could do anything Frank thought I could.

Oh, yes, about my little bear. I had stayed at the ranger station to do some cooking while Frank went up into Lost country. There he came across a she-bear with three cubs. She put one of the cubs up a tree and ran off with the other two. Frank couldn't resist capturing the third and bringing her down to me. We stayed in the hills for about two weeks before we came back home again to Blyn. In that time the cub had accepted me as her mother. I kept her at home until the time came for me to go back to college. If Woodland Park had been as fine as it is now, I probably would have given her to them, but finally decided it would be better to take her into the woods behind the house. There still were huckleberries on the bushes, the woods were full of downed logs teeming with ants and our orchard had windfall apples on the ground. At that time I had long hair and sometimes wore it in a bun in back held with hairpins. She use to love to sit in my lap and pick the pins out of my hair until it hung down.

That last day I took her into the woods until I found a downed rotten log. It was full of ants. I took off her collar and chain and held her in my lap. By that time she was quite big and barely fit. She took the hairpins out of my hair and let it down. I put her onto the log and left her scooping up ants. My mother said theat she came back several times for apples. She said that she looked well-kept. Of course I never saw her again. I would never capture a wild thing again, but I do cherish memories of the time I had her, and it does give me status with my grandchildren.

MOUNTAINS, CAMERAS, AND SCOUTING
or
How The Seeds Were Planted

by Ira Spring

In 1930 Eastman Kodak celebrated their 50th Anniversary by giving a box brownie to every 12-year-old boy and girl in the U.S.A. The Kodak dealer in Shelton was a bit perplexed about giving two cameras to one family. But when it was explained that Bob and I were twins, with due ceremony he presented a camera to both of us. ...

That same year we also joined the Boy Scouts and went to scout camp on Lower Lena Lake for ten days. To get there we rode a truck from Shelton. The first three miles were paved, then over winding gravel road along Hood Canal to Eldon at the mouth of the Hamma Hamma River. There we transferred to a Hamma Hamma logging company railroad speeder and rode the tracks eight miles to the Lena Creek trailhead. In 1930, our first year at camp, the hillside at the beginning of the trail was being logged, so we were led straight up the hill on a fire line. It was a killer. Our packs were as big as we were and much too heavy being full of all the extra clothes and blankets our mother was sure we needed. By the time we reached the regular trail, we tenderfoots were completely pooped out. We all eventually staggered up the two-mile-long trail to camp, but it was a tough trip.

Camp Cleland, as the camp was called, consisted of a large cookhouse, a canvas-covered eating area, and ten army tents. There was a dock and eight rowboats that had been carried up the trail by the older scouts. There was only one woman in camp, the cook, and because of the problems of getting there, no visitors.

The camp periods were 10 days, plenty of time for activities. Merit badges were worked on, but mostly emphasis was on swimming and hiking. No one had a swim suit. It was a little embarrassing to swim in sight of the cookhouse, but then she was an "old lady" and didn't count—probably 35 or 40. As tenderfoots we had a number of day hikes and one overnight hike to Upper Lena Lake. We were impressed and returned to the camp for the next four or five summers. Bob and I had a paper route and saved our allowance all winter so we could have two periods at camp. I got on an advanced crew and helped build cabins to replace the old army tents. ...

What made Camp Cleland so great were the hiking and the leaders. Tom Martin, a school teacher, was one of the greatest personalities I have ever known. He was wonderful with the boys, a great storyteller, had a strong sense of honesty, and loved to hike and fish. ... There were other good leaders. Tom Hardy took over when Tom Martin left teaching school. There were a number of assistant leaders; the most outstanding were Norman Bright, a 1932 Olympic marathon runner, and Chet Ullin, a mountain climber.

By today's standards our backpacking equipment was pretty crude. Bob and I each made our own pack boards from patterns we found in *Boy's*

Life, the scouting magazine. Mother made us each a nice warm (but much too heavy) sleeping bag from a quilt, and with her help we each made pup tents that were waterproof when it didn't rain.

The scout leaders were divided on what we should wear on our feet. They hadn't heard of tricouni nails which were popular in Europe, and "Bramani" (later called Vibram) hadn't been invented yet. Hobnails were slippery on rock and rubber soles were slippery on snow and mud. There had been a serious accident the year before using hobnails, so most of the boys wore shoes with rubber soles.

After our tenderfoot year, Bob and I got to do three-, four-, and even five-day hikes. My most memorable trip was with Chet Ullin as a leader. We hiked the first day to Upper Lena Lake surrounded by alpine meadows and steep mountains. The next day we left the trail and climbed over Mt. Baldy (now on the U.S.G.S. maps as Mt. Lena), then traversed miles of alpine meadows, and ended the day by climbing up over a 6,000 foot pass near the top of Mt. Stone and dropping down to Lake of the Angels surrounded by glacier-polished rock. Chet Ullin had been this far before and helped name the lake, but from here on Chet pioneered a new route across mountain passes and through miles of meadows covered with heather and huckleberries. On the side of Mt. Henderson we accidentally stampeded a herd of 50 or more elk. They came thundering down the mountainside 100 feet in front of us, raising such a cloud of dust we could hardly see the animals. With some route finding problems, we camped the third night at Mildred Lakes. On the fourth day Chet led us under the sharp spires of the Sawtooth Range, past Mt. Washington to a final camp on Jefferson Lake. On the last day we found a trail leading to Elk Lake and a logging road. ...

THREE PRUNE CREEK
The Seattle Mountaineers' Olympic Outing of 1913
by Rudo Fromme

The United States Forest Service controlled all the Olympic Mountain interior until the National Park Service took command of the 'hole in the doughnut' park we know today. Rudo Fromme was an early forest supervisor in those pre-park days. Fromme obtained his master's degree from the Yale University School of Forestry, he began a lifetime career with the Forest Service and came to the Olympics at age 26. During his 1913-1916 tenure much of the trail system was developed. The following excerpt from his memoirs displays his unrelenting humor and also illustrates the role of recreation in the development of the trail system in the Olympic Mountains.

— *Russell Dalton*

Here's probably as good a place as any for some notes on this first crossing of the Olympic Mountains north and south by pack horses or by any sizeable party. There were 115 in this party and they used 35 pack horses, two of which had to be shot, due to serious injuries from rolling down steep canyon slopes. The horses carried only bedding, cooking and special mountain climbing equipment, and supplies. Personal items of toiletry and clothing were carried on foot.

A fair trail was available up to the Elwha River through the Dodwell-Rixon Pass for climbing Mt. Olympus and also to the Low Divide at the head of the North Fork Quinault. The south route, however, was not known to have ever been fully traversed by horse. Grant Humes, a trapper and guide of the lower Elwha, was largely responsible for the passability of the Elwha trail and served as a packer, furnishing some of the horses for this trip. Forest Service trail money was pretty scarce, but I managed to get a small crew working up the North Fork Quinault in the spring to cut a way through the larger down trees and scrape out switch back trails in and out of deep canyon crossings.

Of the 115 Mountaineers on this trip, there were slightly more women than men, and they walked probably 80 miles, not counting the side trips for exploration and mountain climbing. They finished with a dugout canoe trip of about 35 miles down the lower Quinault from the lake of that name to Taholah on the ocean. Indians from the reservation in that location did most of the piloting, or poling.

Kimta Creek Complicates Conditions

We reached Kimta Creek, about six miles from the Low Divide camp, on the way out (third week); it was found necessary to unpack the horses because of insufficient tread and pack clearance.

While some of the men hikers led the horses singly down into this steep canyon and out again on the other side, others back-packed the heavy bed rolls, etc. making several trips per man. The women, of which my wife, Ruby was one (we having hiked in late to catch them on the last two weeks of the outing) all went ahead to make night camp at a certain planned creek, probably two miles below. Two groups of seven or eight horses each with packer and cooks were also sent ahead about mid-afternoon, after repacking with mostly food supplies and cooking equipment, but also some bedding. The rest of the men and horses decided that they had had enough for one day, besides it was getting dark. Three of us decided to push on with the women.

Three Women Worshippers Push On

With flash lights spotting the dim trail ahead, we encountered a makeshift camp of one group of horses and packer about half way. It was Grant Humes. He explained that his horses were falling down at every uncut "cross-log" instead of jumping or stepping high and he was tired of picking them up. He thought that the one group ahead of him had most of the grub anyway. With this assurance we stumbled on. I was in the lead, still wearing my chummy pack sack, containing double sized sleeping bag and leftovers of Swedish hardtack, German erbswurst and dried fruits. As we suddenly faced a series of short switchbacks looking down into a brightly burning bonfire surrounded by about 60 of the feminine gender, singing their hearts out, an evil inspiration took hold of one of us, probably me. I turned to the other two and said, "Just as they finish this song, let's act as though we're herding a bunch of pack horses."

This Fiendish Form of Humor Takes Fire, Then Backfires

"Giddap there, Prince." "Hi Muley" and other such horse herding terms exploded from our diabolical diaphragms as we kicked the dust and gravel about. What a reaction! The black woods for miles around reverberated to feminine screams and squeals of delight. It was just too intense. It not only shattered the woods, but shattered our nerves. It shook us into sudden, startling silence. We stopped stone still, contemplating the cowardly act of sneaking back to be enfolded in the friendy darkness of night. The silence continued ominously. "Can it be that their food didn't come through?" thought we. But, with another wicked hunch, we decided to move on naturally, and to profess absolute ignorance of any pack horse demonstration, blaming their assumption onto hallucinations brought on by desperation. Up to greet us came several of the sprightlier gals; their first questions, peering eagerly into the darkness behind us, "Where are the pack horses?" "We haven't seen any except a bunch we left bedded down a mile back You must be so lonesome or hungry that you are having delusions." "Oh, no! How could you play such a cruel joke—if it could be called a joke." Etc, etc.

The Rivulet Gets Christened "Three Prune Creek"

When we had sneaked around to the back of the cook fly, we learned to our surprise and chagrin that these first eight horses had carried nothing but bedding, except for some pots and pans and one bag of dried prunes, which the cook had already put to soak. Counting them carefully, we found that we could allow three each to the sadly betrayed women and cook crew of three men. While passing around the pails for each to dip in for her dole, I stated in a noble tone that, in punishment for our recent dereliction, the three of us practical jokers were going without prunes, and in that the division would come out without fractions. "Oh, no!" spoke up one or two generous souls, "Have one of mine." "No! No!" protested I. Then I sneaked off with my wife and my two late hiking companions to banquet (by comparison) on my variety of packsack leftovers from our catching up hike of the first week.

The National Geographic Board accepted my explanation for renaming this creek "Three Prune." Can't recall the original designation, but it could have as well been called "Shivering Women Creek."

The bedding carried by these advance horses was not sufficient for full beds around, so they sat huddled around the fire wrapped two or three in one blanket.

The Mountaineers

MOONRISE AND SUNSET, DEER PARK, 1975

A pinnacle
is a clearing, a moment
swept clean of all
but the cougar's cough.
Around us glaciers give way
to Olympic peaks— the upswept basalt
of an earth that swells
and crawls its thick ropes
toward the pure blue of altitude.

We have come
to find out how small
the Self is. We'll sleep in the pitch
black of canvas and whispering
all night, but first
we want a view. It is just July,
and deer who know the simultaneity
of hunger and dusk have almost
brushed our faces in their desire
for yellow blooms.
We stand like statues of ourselves,
inured to wind.

Until the moon,
inching its own burden of snow aloft,
balances. The sun,
in direct opposition,
lingers for a moment
before falling into the Pacific.
To the north a child's atlas
spreads out its green and blue
legend of land and water.
The world at sea level is steeped
in rose. A corner of refracted sun
shivers. We pull our jackets closed,
pivot south toward Mt. Olympus
and the cold.

— *Judith Skillman*

MT. ANGELES IN THE SNOW

Each foot prints a trail into motion
stumbles in boot treads, this climb
from forest to summit with rope burns
and pick axe. Tuft grass, those pines,
white circles weighted with frost.
Tree antlers dive and rear,
flurries like mist sprinkle.
My gaze sifts through light
snow to mountain raw with glacier.
Like them I cling to rock
that never descends, leave my mark
to seek again when colors spring loose.

The rope tugs upward as I slip
into white one could almost nestle.
Bundled tight, baby-face
bared to all around, lifted
up towards someone bigger,
raising my head to see
the whole range slipping
past memory, white mountain zigzagging
into clouds. Up here the world dives
by peaks, as memory slides
into the unretrievable.
I swear I hear singing.

— *Maria Sclafani*

NEAR KALALOCH

for Barbara

Throw sand dollars and they sail alive.
One dead salmon slides to immediate maggots
and the long starch of his side begins,
the chunk of belly gone in teeth
beyond the sonar stab, in green too thick
for signals from our eyes. Tan foam tumbles
and we call the bourbon in us wind.

We put this day in detente with a pastoral
anxiety for stars. Remember when our eyes
were ocean floors and the sun was dissonant
and cold, unlike today. Scream at waves
go back you fools or die, and say once
light was locked in a horizoned hunger.

A crack wind breaks the driftwood's white
from stark to cream. East is lost
but serious with lines: defeated slant
of grass, the cirrus pointed and the sudden
point of sun, the lean of ocean
on our throats, bacon-baited knocks
of sea perch in our palms.

Now the shore is speared by ancient orange,
let a trickle say a beach is bleeding.
Tonight the sea will come like the eyes
of all cats in the world stampeding.

— *Richard Hugo*

DOUBLE ENTRY

Up back from here
are mountains—*the*
mountains.

As a boy, I'd sit
on the porch
on Caroline Street
and glass the mountains
with field glasses, the old
aviator type, not
powerful—but good enough.

Mountain men, goats
and animal tracks.
I'd spot them.

Workers in our town,
no mountain climbers—
just workers in the
woods and mills.
No one to answer what
was back of
those mountains.

My father tried, but
he was tired—the docks,
ships and piles of sulfur.
He never looked up
toward the mountains.
How could he dream
what lay behind?

Trails led into
the mountains.
I took one—climbed to
the highest peak and
looked down—
fog.

Then it lifted and
there was our town.
I began to jump
and holler there above
timberline where a man
can see both ways.
I waved my arms
just in case some
boy was sitting
studying mountains.

Then I lay down
on a rock and dug
my fingers knuckle deep
into the moss and lichen,
the moisture there and
my resting—so I could go

down from this mountain
and tell my children
of mountains and beyond those
the mountains only mountains
can see—all the bright days,
the long clear nights.

— *Morris Bond*

ON A PHOTO OF POP AT HURRICANE RIDGE WITH HIS BOW AND ARROW

this photo has been in our house for as long as i can remember
and it's the way i know i'll always think of you pop standing
there looking up and holding that bow i don't know what it was
you were shooting at and you say now you don't think it was
anything and i guess that's partly why i like it since it seems
that i've spent so much of my life not quite knowing what i'm
shooting at either like maybe it helps me to see that you haven't
always been in quite so much control of things like you haven't
had quite so clear a vision of things as i've sometimes thought
you have

clive mccloud you said took this picture around 32 or 33 you
aren't sure but it was a couple of years before you bought the
grocery store and around a year after the road was built
you can see the road back there to the ridge the old whiskey bend
road that came out at idaho camp anyway you and don feeley were

up there shooting you'd driven up in your old 31 ford coupe just
to spend the day what were you looking for up there well anything
that moved you said and you recalled that old coupe with the
crank on the windshield and how you could move that windshield up
and down or up only and get fresh air in and also shoot right out
the front in case you came across anything that looked good like
maybe a deer or a rabbit or even a marmot though as you recall
those critters were always protected but old clive showed up he
worked for marcheevies or macheesies studio here in town and said
he would send this photo to a post card company but you never did
see the post card if there even was one but what did happen was
that when you got married a couple of years later old clive sent you
this for a wedding present

now you've lost both legs and don't stand so tall as you did back
then when even those mountains couldn't shorten you when you
stood right up to the most majestic of any mountain when you had
no me and no mom no irene dave dan when all you had was that
great hat cocked to one side and that long stemmed pipe tight
between your teeth and that doug fairbanks mustache and those
baggy cords and that 31 coupe and those mountains and that aim
that aim that long unhampered and nothing but the world out
there aim and now you laugh and talk about clive and don and you
get up and show us how you can walk on those false legs and you say
it's just like walking on stilts

— *Jack Estes*

LAST DAY OF SUMMER ON
HURRICANE RIDGE

Long abandoned, the old road blocked with sunken post
leads down to Whiskey Bend
and the elk river, Elwha, far below.
Cushioned clumps
of Pearly Everlasting, papery now,
are strewn along its bed,
and the limber, rubber young of Alpine Fir.

Part way down
we climb the shale slope
through brown bracken,
bent in a cascade over the bank,
past podded lupine
and the brown collapsed wreaths
of cow parsnip,
through grass combed by the run-off snow.

A day for marmots in the sun.
Like old men on park benches,
they know how it should be spent;
asleep, content, in their summer coats.
So we lie down in grass in grain
near the dun-colored soil
at the mouths of marmot holes;
lie so still that they close their lids
over black shiny eyes,
before their long night.

Old trees creak their branches
in the wind that rustles hollow parsnip stalks.
The drone of a distant plane
blends with fly and grasshopper crossfire.
Canada jays demand from picnickers,
and under it all sounds
the "yank-yank" of the nuthatch.

Inner glaciers hoard the snow.
Haze settles in the breast-like ridges
and the dark-shadowed firs,
their frosted upright cones
sugary-looking in the sun,
stand black against Olympics.

We climb back up the gravel road.
The late sun warms our backs.
Old marmots whistle to their young.
Where strawberry's red runners
stitch the ground,
I stoop to test young firs
against the weight of snow,
on an old road not meant to last,
overrun with Everlasting.

— *Frances Fagerlund*

AT THE LAKE WITHOUT L.

Lines climb toward sunken weeds
where earth continues, bone beneath
the liquid eye. Somewhere fish
are not seeing our bait as we
cannot watch morning grow old;
but we paddle imaginary latitudes
hoping for one needle-thin trout.

*

Two boats, resting like spoons on jelly,
three men too far for eye to eye, no
language stitches the still air among
us. But that is understood as, briefly,
we stare across opaque water larger
than any floor and (it is easy) look away.

*

Two herons share the water's near
edge, patrolling, living. Ashore,
friends move within their lakes of sleep,
unaware of navigation, of intent;
though we, in our own sleeps, are not far.

The herons too are undisturbed
in their world of water above and below.
What we are to them, motions,
Leanne, I am to you.

*

Current, the wind: the dream dresses
itself in language. We know we exist,
we know why, but only here—
a huge cell's nucleus, perhaps;
we reel in and cast, know only
everything we know.

With their purposes, boats
ignore each other: the *pas de deux*
abstractly goes on.

— *Sean Bentley*

Epilogue

Humes Ranch
May 18, 1925

Asahel Curtis
Seattle, Wash.

Dear Asahel:

I have just returned from Port Angeles, (first time I have been in *any* town in 16 months) where I heard Mr. Fromme give his illustrated talk on the Olympics before the Elks club. ...

The pictures were enjoyed by about 100 men and were instructive as far as they went. Personally, I would have liked to see more of your *new* series and less of the old ones which have been shown here several times before by Webster and others—products of such local scrubs as Billy Everett, myself and a few others. ...

Grant Humes and Montelius Price on Mt. Queets, 1907

Taking up paragraph four of your letter, I quote: "Of course, the farther we get the road the better and I am still of the opinion that we will live long enough to see a road through the range."

In this view I do not concur, even tho it would possibly enhance the value of my property; and I am now, always was and always shall be opposed to *highways* through the heart of the Olympics. When the Olympic Highway is completed, that is as far as roads need to go in this range. It is not so large but what, with improved trails, people could leave their cars for a few hours or days, and on horseback enjoy the interior in a way far more pleasing and of lasting benefit to them than from the interior of a rushing slaughter-wagon which gives no time to see anything except the dust from other vehicles—also rushing. The time has come for this generation to pause and take stock. What heritage are we going to pass along to the generations yet unborn? Shall it be jackrabbits to hunt, tadpoles to fish and blackened desolation where our green, cool, water-conserving forests are now?

All one needs is to look about him in other fields to see the handwriting on the wall, see what railroads and auto roads have done to the landscape and the wild things thereof. If we don't look out, we of the United States will soon have to flee to Canada when we desire to sojurn in the unspoiled, "Great Open Spaces."

And this is why I am on record, as stated above, in this matter. ...

Cordially,
Grant Humes

Grant Humes and his "right hand man"

Contributors

HORACE ALBRIGHT was director of the National Park Service and profoundly influenced its policies and development. His books include: *Oh Ranger* and *The Birth of the National Park Service.*

JEREMY ANDERSON was a native of Washington. Educated at Yale and the University of Washington, he was professor of geography at Eastern Washington University. He died in a climbing accident in October of 1987.

MICHEL BATISSE was formerly Deputy Assistant Director of the Science Sector of UNESCO. He lives in Paris, France.

MARVIN BELL is author of eight books of poetry, a book of essays and (with William Stafford) a collection of poems written as correspondence. He lives in Port Townsend, WA, as much as possible, and also in Iowa City, Iowa.

BETH BENTLEY's poems have appeared in over a hundred literary journals and anthologies. She received a Writer's Fellowship from the National Endowment of the Arts and was awarded the Montalvo Achievement in Poetry award. She teaches poetry for the University of Washington.

NELSON BENTLEY is a professor of English at the University of Washington. His books include *Iron Man of the Hoh, Sea Lion Caves, Moose Call, Snoqualmie Falls Apocalypse.* Forthcoming are *Selected Poems* and *Tracking the Transcendental Moose.*

SEAN BENTLEY is associate editor for Madrona Publishers, co-editor of *Fine Madness magazine,* a songwriter and poet. His books include *Instances* and *Into the Bright Oasis.*

BRYN BEORSE is a writer and photographer for the *Aberdeen Daily World.* He studied photography at Western Washington University and was involved in the rebuilding of the Chalet at Enchanted Valley.

NANCY BERES was born and raised on the Olympic Peninsula. Her work has appeared in *Tidepools, The Berkeley Review,* and *Tablets the Rain Inscribes,* a Northwest Renaissance Anthology.

MORRIS BOND lives in Sequim and works as a timber cutter.

BRUCE BROWN's book *Mountain in the Clouds* (Simon and Schuster) is an eloquent plea for the preservation of the Northwest's wild salmon runs. He lives with his wife in the Fraser Valley.

KAREN LULL-BUTLER, a Port Townsend, WA resident, has a degree in fisheries technology. She has done textile printing and illustrations of Northwest plants and animals.

MIKE BUTLER, a resident of Port Townsend, WA, is an electronics technician by trade. His hobbies include drawing, model trains, and restoration of his Victorian home.

RAYMOND CARVER, award-winning poet, screenwriter, and author of short stories, calls Port Angeles, WA his home. He is on leave from a teaching position at Syracuse University in New York.

MITZI CHANDLER lives in Port Angeles, WA with her husband. Her writing includes children's plays, magazine articles and poetry. Her first book of poems, *Whiskey's Song*, was released in August 1987.

ROBERT CHANDLER has been with the National Park Service for twenty-nine years. He has served as Superintendent of Olympic National Park for five years.

LOIS BROWN CRISLER was a creative writing instructor at the University of Washington and married to Herb Crisler, a professional photographer and mountaineer. Her writings championed wilderness and understanding of the wolf. Her books include *Arctic Wild* and *Captive Wild*.

ASAHEL CURTIS was a well-known Northwest commercial photographer, mountain guide, founder of the (Seattle) Mountaineers, and promoter of commerce and development.

MICHAEL DALEY is a poet and teacher living in Seattle. His collection of poems, *The Straits*, is published by Empty Bowl.

RUSSELL DALTON is a Port Angeles, WA native and a student of Olympic Mountain history. He has worked in Olympic National Park seasonally as fire guard, ranger, naturalist, and is presently on the trail crew.

ALICE DERRY teaches English at Peninsula College in Port Angeles, WA. Her first collection, *Stages of Twilight*, appeared from Breitenbush in 1986.

IVAN DOIG lives in Seattle. He is the celebrated author of several books, including *Winter Brothers*, *This House of Sky*, and *English Creek*.

WILLIAM O. DOUGLAS was the longest-seated Supreme Court Justice in history. A native of Washington, he led conservationists in blocking proposed highway developments in the Olympic National Park. His books include *Of Men and Mountains* and *Beyond the High Himalayas*.

JACK ESTES teaches literature, popular culture, and video production at Peninsula College in Port Angeles, WA, his home town.

SENATOR DANIEL J. EVANS is a former Governor of Washington and the former President of Evergreen State College. He has been a long-time supporter of Olympic National Park.

FRANCES FAGERLUND was born in Logan, UT, where she graduated from Utah State University. She lives with her husband, Gunnar, in Dungeness, WA.

GUNNAR O. FAGERLUND entered the National Park Service in 1934, and served at several locations from Yellowstone to Hawaii. In addition to botanizing and doing photography, he was Olympic National Park's first chief naturalist.

LENA FLETCHER was the eldest daughter of Hoh pioneers John and Dora Huelsdonk. For many years she wrote a column for the *Forks Forum,* recollecting pioneer life and peppering it with comments on contemporary rural life and dealing with bureaucracies.

DAVID //// (FORLINES) is a Native American artist who carved the ridgepole at Kalaloch Lodge, in Kalaloch, WA, and teaches carving at La Push, WA.

RUDO FROMME was an early Forest Supervisor back when the U. S. Forest Service controlled all the Olympic Mountain interior. He received his master's degree from the Yale University School of Forestry.

ED HARKNESS grew up in Seattle and teaches English at Shoreline and Edmonds Community Colleges. He's published two chapbooks of poetry: *Long Eye Lost Wind Forgive Me* and *Fiddle Wrapped in a Gunny Sack.*

DOLLY STEARNS HARMAN must remain an enigma. No biographical information could be found. Her books include: *Peak Shadows* and *The Duchess o' Something or Other.*

JACK HENSON was a writer for the *Port Angeles Evening News* for many years.

RICHARD HUGO was a native of Washington and placed the settings for many of his poems on the Olympic Peninsula. His collected poems, *Making Certain It Goes On,* is published by W.W. Norton.

RUBY EL HULT was born in Idaho and has been writing all her life. Her works include *Untamed Olympics, Steamboats in the Timber,* and *Northwest Disasters.* She resides in Puyallup, WA and has many writing projects under way.

GRANT HUMES pioneered on the upper Elwha for thirty-five years, packing and guiding. After his death, Herb and Lois Crisler lived at the homestead for ten years. The Humes' cabin is now on the National Register of Historic Places.

STEVEN R. JOHNSON, a Port Townsend resident, studied photography at Western Washington State College under Dr. Rice. His photographs have appeared in several Empty Bowl publications, most notably, *Here Among the Sacrificed.*

CAROLE KAHLER's lifelong interest in art and drawing led to a double major in art and biology. Since 1972, she has been a free-lance illustrator of signs and brochures for Olympic National Park.

BOB KAUNE worked with Olympic National Park from 1965 to 1982 as a park naturalist and backcountry management specialist. He and his family are long-time residents of the Peninsula and avid users of the Olympic National Park wilderness.

RICK LANDRY was born in Forks, WA and was raised on a Hoh riverfront farm. He now works in greenhouse agriculture.

CARSTEN LEIN is a conservationist and long-time supporter of Olympic National Park. He is presently working on an administrative history of Olympic National Park.

SVANTE LOFGREN was from Sweden and a friend of K. O. Erickson. He is the author of *Barth Arkel*, which is the biography of Erickson.

HARVEY MANNING is a dedicated conservationist and one of the deans of outdoor writing in the Northwest. He is the author of *Washington Wilderness: The Unfinished Work* from which his essay was excerpted, and more recently, *Walking the Beach to Bellingham*.

TIM McNULTY is a poet, conservationist and nature writer who lives in the foothills country of the northeast Olympics. He has co-authored, with photographer Pat O'Hara, an award-winning series of books on our wilderness national parks published by Woodlands Press.

EDMOND S. MEANY came to Washington Territory in 1877. He was a principal in organizing the Press expedition into the Olympics. His books include: *Mountain Camp Fires* (poetry), *History of the State of Washington, Indian Geographic Names of Washington,* and *Origin of Geographic Names.*

PHYLLIS MILETICH is a free-lance writer, a feature columnist for the *Peninsula Daily News* and a teacher of writing. She has published two books, raised five children and now lives with her husband on the Olympic Peninsula.

MURRAY MORGAN has been teaching and writing about Pacific Northwest history for forty years. His book, *The Last Wilderness*, is available through the University of Washington Press.

KENYON NATTINGER was born and raised in Port Angeles, WA and now teaches part-time at Peninsula College.

BONNIE NELSON was born in Forks, WA. Her poetry has been published in the *Bellingham Review, Blue Unicorn, Cedar Rock, Cutbank, Kansas Quarterly, Poetry Seattle* and others.

MICHAEL O'CONNOR is a poet and Peninsula native. His book *The Rainshadow* (Empty Bowl) is a beautiful evocation of the Dungeness Valley. For the past eight years he has been living in Taipei, China.

PAT O'HARA is a Puget Sound native. Since he began a full-time career in photography in late 1978, his photographs have been widely published. His work has received critical acclaim from, among others, the *American Photographer* magazine and the Society of Professional Journalists.

LLOYD S. (SMITTY) PARRATT is a ranger-naturalist in Olympic National Park. He and his wife, Shawn, were the first couple, and she the first woman, to hike all 675 miles of trail in the park, including the entire coastal strip and all major cross-country traverses. He has published a book on place names of Olympic National Park.

BEN PHILLIPS came to Port Angeles in 1913 and began a life-long career in banking. In 1915, he helped found the Klahhane Club, an outdoor and hiking club that still enjoys and supports the wilderness of the Olympic Peninsula.

GIFFORD PINCHOT was an early 20th century conservationist in America, and the first chief of the United States Forest Service. He first visited the Olympic Peninsula in 1897.

BILL RANSOM was one of the founders of Centrum, a center for cultural arts in Port Townsend, WA. His books of poetry include *Finding True North* and *The Single Man Looks at Winter*. His fiction work includes two novels written with Frank Herbert, *The Jesus Incident* and *The Lazarus Effect*. *The Ascension Factor* was published in 1987.

THEODORE ROETHKE was a Pulitzer Prize-winning poet who taught for many years at the University of Washington. His *Collected Poems* are published by Doubleday. He died in 1963.

STEVE SANFIELD is a professional storyteller as well as a poet. Author of *Wandering* and *A New Way*, his most recent book is *A Natural Man: The True Story of John Henry*.

MARIA SCLAFANI's manuscript, *Familiar Reunion,* won the University of Washington Grayston Award in 1986. In 1987 she was runner-up for the Milliman Scholarship. Her work has appeared in *The Seattle Review, The Pegasus Anthology* and others.

JUDITH SKILLMAN lives in Bellevue, WA with her husband and three children. Her collection, *The Worship of the Visible Spectrum,* was selected for the King County Arts Commission 1987 Publication Prize.

GARY SNYDER was raised in rural Washington State. He has published 13 books of poetry and prose. *Turtle Island* won the Pulitzer Prize for poetry in 1975.

IRA SPRING and his twin brother grew up in Shelton, WA. In 1928, they followed their father on their first hike in the Olympics, which became a yearly event. It was these hikes that led to a love of mountains and a career in photography.

ROBERT SUND is a poet, painter and calligrapher whose work is steeped in and nutured by his native northwest landscape. His books of poems include *Bunch Grass* (University of Washington Press) and *Ish River* (North Point Press). He lives in LaConner, WA.

ANNETTE CHADDOCK SWAN was the illustrator of the E. B. Webster books: *The Friendly Mountain* (second edition) and *Fishing in the Olympics.*

MARIAN TAYLOR was a packer in the Olympics for many years. Camp Marian on the Dosewallips is named for her. She currently lives in Blyn, WA.

KEITH THOMPSON settled on the Olympic Peninsula in 1910. He hiked extensively in the Olympics and knew many of the pioneer homesteaders. He practiced dentistry in Port Angeles, WA for 50 years.

EDWARD TISCH is biology-botany instructor at Peninsula College in Port Angeles, WA. He is a poet, Japanese gardener, and has co-authored papers on Olympic flora.

JAMIE VALADEZ grew up on the Lower Elwha near Port Angeles. She is a student of Klallam Indian folklore and has compiled a collection of Native American legends.

WILLARD VAN NAME committed his whole life to saving trees. His pamphlet, *The Proposed Olympic National Park*, is credited as the major force in the creation of Olympic National Park.

LISA VOILAND is from Colorado, trained in art at University of Colorado and Evergreen State College. She has lived at Kalaloch, WA off and on for the past fifteen years.

CHARLOTTE GOULD WARREN has drawn and written since high school. Published most recently in *The Literary Review* and *Kansas Quarterly*, she grew up in India and has lived for the past 23 years in Dungeness, WA.

CHARLES N. WEBSTER was the son and successor of Port Angeles, WA publisher E. B. Webster. He directed a series of crusades for community betterment, one of which supported the establishment of Olympic National Park.

E. B. WEBSTER was an early owner of the *Port Angeles Evening News* and co-founder of Klahhane Club. An avid botanist, he discovered an endemic flower on Mount Angeles and wrote extensively about the Olympics.

GEORGE WELCH: Port Townsend, WA resident and civic leader. He was an active climber, hiker, and photographer who ranged the Olympics from Hood Canal to Olympus to the coast during the early years of this century.

JAMES WICKERSHAM was a probate judge, an attorney for the city of Tacoma and a member of Washington's state legislature. He made the first known proposal for Olympic National Park in November, 1890.

ROBERT L. WOOD is a dedicated student of Olympic history, and a persistent backcountry explorer. The most recent of his many books about the Olympics is *Olympic Mountains Trail Guide* published by The Mountaineers.

Cover design by The Zimmerman Group

Interior design by The Zimmerman Group and Cynthesis Graphic Design

Formatting and production by Cynthesis Graphic Design. Composed on a Macintosh Plus™ computer in 10 point Palatino on 11 leading, using *Pagemaker*® and converted to final type on an Allied Linotronic 300™. Display type composed by The Type Gallery in Pistilli bold.

Printed and bound by MacNaughton & Gunn on 50# offset.

Illustrators and photographers:

Turn of the Seasons

p. 1	CAROLE KAHLER
p. 5	GUNNAR FAGERLUND
p. 10	GUNNAR FAGERLUND
p. 12	GUNNAR FAGERLUND

Origins

p. 15	CAROLE KAHLER
p. 18	LISA VOILAND
p. 23	CHARLOTTE WARREN
p. 26	STEVE R. JOHNSON
p. 31	STEVE R. JOHNSON

Explorations

p. 33	ANNETTE CHADDOCK SWAN
p. 38	NATIONAL PARK SERVICE
p. 48	GEORGE WELCH
p. 51	RUSS DALTON COLLECTION

Controversy

p. 61	KAREN LULL-BUTLER
p. 64	CAROLE KAHLER
p. 65	CAROLE KAHLER
p. 69	CAROLE KAHLER
p. 74	GEORGE WELCH
p. 79	ANNETTE CHADDOCK SWAN

Pioneers

p. 85	MICHAEL BUTLER
p. 100	KAREN LULL-BUTLER
p. 103	GUNNAR FAGERLUND
p. 105	BRYN BEORSE

Wilderness

p. 107	CAROLE KAHLER
p. 113	GERRY HUMES COLLECTION
p. 115	STEVE R. JOHNSON
p. 117	CAROLE KAHLER
p. 121	CAROLE KAHLER
p. 127	PHOTOGRAPHER UNKNOWN
p. 135	GUNNAR FAGERLUND
p. 137	RUSS DALTON COLLECTION
p. 138	KAREN LULL-BUTLER
p. 139	KAREN LULL-BUTLER

Memoirs

p. 145	ANNETTE CHADDOCK SWAN
p. 149	UNIVERSITY OF WASHINGTON ARCHIVES
p. 153	TOM RULSON
p. 160	GERRY HUMES COLLECTION
p. 166	PHOTOGRAPHER UNKNOWN
p. 171	ASAHEL CURTIS
p. 172	GEORGE WELCH